Y0-AQL-057

Philip J. Fox is vice president of a major investment banking firm and has assisted numerous small businesses. Joseph R. Mancuso, an internationally known author and entrepreneur, is currently the Director of the Center for Entrepreneurial Management, Inc., a not-for-profit educational organization that champions the cause of the entrepreneurial manager.

402

things you must know before starting a new business

philip j. fox
joseph r. mancuso

A SPECTRUM BOOK

Prentice-Hall, Inc., Englewood Cliffs, N.J. 07632

Library of Congress Cataloging in Publication Data

Fox, Philip J
    402 things you must know before starting your own business.

    (A Spectrum Book)
    Includes index.
    1. Small business—Management.   2. Self-employed.
I. Mancuso, Joseph, joint author.   II. Title.
HD69.S6F69   658.1'141   79-27894
ISBN 0-13-329136-7
ISBN 0-13-329128-6 pbk.

Editorial production/supervision by Shirley Covington
Manufacturing buyer: Cathie Lenard

10 9 8 7 6 5 4 3 2 1

Printed in the United States of America

PRENTICE-HALL INTERNATIONAL, INC., *London*
PRENTICE-HALL OF AUSTRALIA PTY. LIMITED, *Sydney*
PRENTICE-HALL OF CANADA, LTD., *Toronto*
PRENTICE-HALL OF INDIA PRIVATE LIMITED, *New Delhi*
PRENTICE-HALL OF JAPAN, INC., *Tokyo*
PRENTICE-HALL OF SOUTHEAST ASIA PTE. LTD., *Singapore*
WHITEHALL BOOKS LIMITED, WELLINGTON, *New Zealand*

Contents

To Our Children

May *Karyn, Amy, Alison* and *Kevin* find as much enjoyment in reading this book as their fathers did in writing it.

Preface

The Small Business Administration estimates that 40% of new companies fail during their first year. Only one in nine new enterprises lasts until its seventh year! To a large extent, survival is based on the groundwork done in the crucial initial planning and development state of a firm. Although there are books on starting a company, no book until now has been written that has presented a concise, clear list of what's important and what works. Our goal in compiling such a list has been to *improve your probability of success* and to help you beat long odds against making it as an entrepreneur.

For many people starting a business offers great potential reward. It is an opportunity to become financially independent and to be their own boss. But starting a new company, it is a little bit like shooting the rapids, hot-air ballooning, or photographing wild animals. It takes a special kind of individual to want to do it. With 76 million Americans employed, it can be expected that if the job attitudes and sense of alienation described in Studs Terkel's Working are representative, numerous new ventures will spring up every year.

This book is for entrepreneurs who want to create an

ongoing business. There are about 10 million businesses in the United States, of which about 9 1/2 million are so-called *small businesses*. These small businesses produce 43% of the business output of the United States, a third of the Gross National Product (GNP), and more than half of all private employment. A special category of small businesspersons, the *entrepreneur*, has given the American economy its direction and thrust since the Civil War. Yet to start a small business from nothing and to finance and manage it require motivation and perseverence bordering on obsession. It also takes a good deal of luck. It's an uphill task at which more people fail than succeed. Some people believe that persons willing to risk so much against such odds (some studies claim that eight out of nine new businesses fail) are crazy, but in the American capitalistic system entrepreneurs are folk heroes.

People who start companies are usually impatient for information, pressed for time to do what they want, and anxious to use whatever shortcuts are available to them. The following chapters have been prepared with this in mind. You can probably read all the numbered, italicized suggestions in the book in about two hours. If you have more time, you may want to read the entire book and then reread the italic material. Or you may decide to read only specific chapters, such as the one on exporting and importing, to fill in gaps in your knowledge. This book can also be used as a reference as your company progresses. To make it more readable, a mythical company is used as an example in each chapter.

Despite the large number of suggestions it makes, the book cannot discuss every possible way of handling a business situation. Many business approaches are difficult to generalize about. Consider, for example, the experience of a friend of mine. Upset at not getting a description of his product accepted for publication in the new-products section of *Playboy*, he stormed out of the editor's office. In the men's room he changed from his business suit into a Superman costume, which he had thoughtfully brought along, and reappeared in the editor's office. "You're in," shouted the astonished editor. You and I could theorize all day as to why that approach worked without reaching any conclusions.

Nevertheless, this book does have something for anyone starting a new business. You should at least consider the suggestions in each chapter, although you may not use them. Many suggestions can be useful directly; others can shorten the decision-making process for you. If you are already in business, you can compare your own ideas with ours.

Luck, timing, and persistence play a large part in any company's development. If you are starting a new company, the chance of success is small, but it is there. If, despite the odds you want to join the band of adventurers known as entrepreneurs, this book will be a valuable guide during your apprenticeship.

one

Developing an idea for a new business

*"Let him step to the music which he hears,
however measured or far away."*

Henry David Thoreau

So you want to start a new company? New companies are started for many reasons. Many are started because two individuals have an idea for a company, and they reinforce and support each other's goals. Occasionally, a new product idea will be so attractive that a new company will be built around it, and a product line will be developed. Success stories of persons who have made $1 million with a particular product or company in the past also encourage new ventures.

Many new businesses begin because the founders are bored with their current jobs and have little idea of the risks and difficulties involved in running a company. Family and friends often challenge an individual to start a business; some new ventures are started simply to prove someone wrong. "You'll never get anywhere with *that* idea" is an all-too-familiar refrain. A friend's comment that many people talk about starting a company, but few actually go through with it, may provide just the impetus a man needs to have incorporation papers drawn up.

The odds against success are long, as the Small Business Administration figures will tell you. At best, it is said that *only one in five* companies started today will still be around five years from now. Nevertheless, a large variety of new products and companies emerge each year. Most of these are started by people hoping to make piles of money, have fun, and generate some excitement in their lives. In this chapter, we shall list many of the things these people should consider before they begin.

Every student of entrepreneurship has speculated about what motivates a man or woman to leave a good job to start his or her own business. Some say that such people are basically insecure and must prove their worth on their own. Some argue that these individuals just can't be happy working for someone else, that they have to be their own boss. Others claim that entrepreneurs spring from the ranks of those bored by the slow pace in a large company and hungry for more action. Still others suggest that they are motivated by a nagging mate or a desire to keep up with the Joneses.

Any or *all* of these factors may influence a person's decision to strike out on his or her own, but more often than not, it is the realization that as long as you're working for someone else, your employer is earning at least 25% more than you are.

Don't be misled. It's not the money that's important to the true entrepreneur so much as the need to decide for himself (or herself) what his (or her) true worth is. The desire to make money is, in fact, a poor reason to go into business. Most successful companies are founded by someone with an idea, a dream. Making money is a byproduct of accomplishing some other goal.

To illustrate the 28 points made in this chapter, we shall use a mythical firm, the Pyramid Construction Company, founded in 3000 B.C. with King Ramses IV of Egypt as president.

Number 1 *The first consideration for any new company is what products to offer.* Most companies begin with a predetermined product. In such fast-moving industries as electronics, a substantial number of new products appear every year. However, in certain industries, it may be difficult to come up with new product ideas as often as every five years.

The product of the Pyramid Construction Company is to be pyramids. With the Egyptian king as company president, acceptance of the product is likely to be high.

Number 2 *For information on a product or an industry, there is no better source than your local library.* Countless letters, interviews, and phone calls can be saved by getting acquainted with the data available in library books and articles.

In 3000 B.C., we would probably have to talk to the local wise men (consultants) since little written material existed.

Number 3 *In doing research, the founder of a new company must learn to categorize material and sort out what is relevant.* However, once the information is sorted out, one can often get an extraordinarily good focus on a particular industry or product. If a company is going to be a service company, there is also a great deal of information about service industries that will be of use.

Since there probably were many Egyptians in 3000 B.C. who considered themselves wise, we would have to sort out those with valuable information. Some worthwhile hieroglyphics might also be available.

Number 4 *Often, a library with a good collection of business publications will have one that deals directly with the kind of product you will be offering.* Usually you can learn about new products by flipping through back issues of a particular industry publication. Magazine advertisements can also tell you what kinds of products are being offered and how competitive your idea will be.

The following four directories of industry publications are those most likely to be available in your local library. The first is the best overall source of assistance.

Bacon's Publicity Checker
14 E. Jackson Blvd.
Chicago, IL 60604
Phone: (312) 922-8419

Ayer's Directory of Newspapers and Periodicals
William J. Luedke, Publisher
Ayer Press
210 West Washington Square
Philadelphia, PA 19106
Phone: (215) 829-4472

The Standard Periodical Directory
Oxbridge Publishing Co.
183 Madison Ave.
Room 1108
New York, NY 10016
Phone: (212) 189-8524

Ulrich's Directory of Periodicals
R. R. Bowker Company
1180 Avenue of the Americas
New York, NY 10036
Phone: (212) 764-5100

It is doubtful that a *Pyramid Construction Magazine* existed in 3000 B.C. However, the town crier might be announcing news of other construction projects . . . dams, mud houses, and the like.

Number 5 *For detailed technical information on products, the most valuable and economical source may be an expert technical advisor.* Often, a professor at a local college or an engineer in a nearby company will agree to provide information for a minimum consulting fee. Occasionally, a consulting fee may run as high as $50 an hour, but one hour of an expert's time may be well worth purchasing for the advice you can obtain. This obviously is a far less expensive route than hiring someone fulltime to do research.

A new federally funded organization has been developed to help small businesses in New England with new product development. This organization, called the New England Application Center (NERAC), has a technical staff of 52 professional researchers with expertise in a wide variety of disciplines. Assistance is free, but it is limited to small business. For help, write to:

NERAC
Mansfield Professional Park
Storrs, CT 06268
Phone: (203) 386-4533

For a free quarterly publication on new product ideas generated as a byproduct of government research, write to:

NASA Tech Briefs
NASA
Director of Technical Utilities
Box 8757
BWI Airport, MD 21240

In 3000 B.C. Pyramid could consult Prince Christopher, a local builder of mud houses and an expert in structures, for only drachmas an hour.

Number 6 *Thinking about how to do some things better or more cheaply is probably the most direct route by which new companies get started.* For example, the president of a West Coast company was riding to Los Angeles Airport in a taxicab when it occurred to him that existing taxicab meters might well be improved by making them operate on the same principle as a digital clock. This idea, the substitution of an improved product for an existing product with an established market, was an excellent basis for a new company. The Pyramid Construction Company also followed this route, planning a substantial improvement on existing methods of burial.

Number 7 *Good marketing information is mandatory when you are thinking of starting a business. Telephone calls are better than letters for securing market information.* A letter written to a large company often takes many weeks to get answered. Our friend with the idea for digital taxicab meters called the Yellow Cab Company in Detroit to find out how many cabs are made each year, thus obtaining, immediately, information that would have taken a long time to find out by letter.

The following table may be helpful in deciding where to look for market information:

Sources of Marketing Information	Quality of Information	Cost of Information
Personal contacts	High	High
Phone contacts	Medium	Medium
Mail contacts	Low	Low

Pyramid talked directly with King Ramses and invited him to be the company president. A marketing trip throughout Egypt showed no existing pyramids.

Number 8 *A reference book called the* THOMAS REGISTER *lists all manufacturers according to their products.* Available in many libraries, this book is a valuable resource. You can often find someone who will make a product for you or find out whether certain products exist. In an early equivalent of the *Thomas Register*, Pyramid found several suppliers of smoothed stone and crushed gravel.

Testing Ideas for New Companies

In deciding whether an idea for a new company is viable, it is often helpful to have some type of checklist.

Number 9 *Anyone with an idea for a new company should think about the following basic questions:*

1. Is the product or service to be offered unique?
2. Is there a large enough market for it?
3. Can financing for project be obtained?
4. Do I really want to do all the work the project will involve?

If the answer to all four of these questions is yes, it is time to proceed to the next stage, to the six decision points in Exhibit 1. Often you will find that if you can't answer yes to all four of the questions above right away, you can do so if you make some slight variation in the product or service to be offered.

In Pyramid's case, no competing products exist, the king is the chief market, and he has said "yes" to the idea. The country's coffers can finance the project, and the king is certain that people can be found to do the work involved.

Major Decision Points in Setting Up a New Firm

Exhibit 1 on page 14 shows the major decision points to consider when starting a new company.

Number 10 *In considering the organization of a firm, much depends on whether a product or a service will be offered.* A product will probably require a substantial amount of inventory financing. A service may require a substantial number of employees.

Pyramid is actually selling a service in the building of pyramids. It is fortunate that its market is well defined.

Number 11 *A decison must also be made about concentrating on industrial or consumer markets.* Everyone is a consumer. For this reason, selling consumer products looks easy to many people. One drawback, however, of consumer products is that few are unique. Large companies can overcome this problem by heavy advertising or maintaining a massive sales force. To compete directly against them is impossible for a small company. Its efforts are a whisper lost in the roar of a football crowd. Unique products often have a chance if they are introduced well by a small company, but they are rare.

Industrial markets may seem easier to break into in some cases, since the main task of many purchasing agents is to

review new products. Often one large company may use enough of a product to entirely support a small company. Usually it is best to base the decision whether to aim for industrial or consumer use on the kind of experience the firm's managers have and the type of service or product being marketed.

Pyramids are definitely a consumer product. Everyone who sees them is impressed by them or enjoys their beauty.

Number 12 *A new company must also consider whether to operate at the retail, wholesale, or manufacturing level.* Operating a retail store often looks like the easiest way to offer a product. You're selling what other people make and many people will call on you to offer you products. To many people, clothing looks like the easiest product to sell. However, there are numerous clothing stores, and extreme caution is advised before opening any type of retail store.

Pyramid Construction is essentially a wholesaler. It will rely on suppliers for rock and gravel and local employment markets for labor. Its skill will be in putting the whole package together to please the king.

Number 13 *Location is an important factor in the success of a retail store.* It's proverbial that three things are important in a retail business: (1) location, (2) location, and (3) location. Since Pyramid's products will be seen by many and are difficult to build, the highly visible land on the bank of the Nile River seems the best location for them.

Number 14 *Since wholesalers can sell either to industrial users or to retail stores, a wholesale company with extensive distribution is a stong possibility for a new business.* If its Egyptian efforts go well, Pyramid may think of opening branch offices throughout the Middle East.

Number 15 *Talking to the owner of an existing business can prevent you from making mistakes, especially in setting up a wholesale company.* Wholesale companies or distributorships often rely on personal contacts for business, and it is important to determine what contacts are necessary to be successful in a particular industry.

There are certain advantages to being a wholesaler. You can sell products from several manufacturers. If products change, you can change manufacturers. Wholesalers deal in finished products. If a particular item doesn't work, back it goes to the manufacturer.

Abe, a local sandal maker, and Job, a local robe dealer, have agreed to review Pyramid's organizational plan.

Number 16 *The principle advantage in starting a manufacturing company is that banks and financial institutions like to see their dollars invested in tangible assets such as plants and equipment.* For a new manufacturing company, the major problem is the length of time it takes to get started operating, and to test products.

If Pyramid had chosen manufacturing as its chief line of business, it would have approached the Bank of Mesopotamia for a loan rather than going to the king.

Number 17 *The principal drawback to manufacturing is the substantial investment in plant and equipment it requires.* Although banks and financial institutions will lend money on manufacturing companies, it is often necessary to pile up large amounts of dollars to get the company off the ground and keep it going.

Had Pyramid opted for manufacturing, its financing requirements would have exceeded the lending capacity of the local bank, the Bank of Mesopotamia.

Number 18 *Much depends on whether a new company will sell its products or services locally, regionally, or nationwide.* The obvious advantage of selling products locally is that you can analyze the market personally. If you have a problem with a customer, you can get in your car, visit the customer, and straighten things out. The principal disadvantage of doing business on a local basis is the relatively small number of potential buyers for your products.

Local operations have several strong advantages. The manager can do most of the selling personally, and delivery expenses are low. There are few long-distance phone calls, and control problems are minimal. You can also develop a good reading of the community, because living in the area lets you personally test what products are required. However, because they can't reach enough people with their products, many local companies aren't attractive to potential investors. These investors look for a company that has a broad geographical base and products that have a possibility of being marketed nationally.

Pyramid is a local company. To move cut stone and boulders nationwide by camel would be a big headache.

Number 19 *Companies marketing on a regional basis should be careful to take into account communities within the region.* Local trends, taste in fashion, and lifestyles may be entirely different and inconsistent within a region, even one as small as a three-state area.

If Pyramid expanded regionally, it would have to take into account the lack of rivers in outlying districts. This would make site location more difficult.

Number 20 *Another major decision for a would-be entrepreneur is whether to purchase a company or start one from scratch.* This is an important decision. To buy a company, you will need to raise funds. If you are inexperienced, you will have a hard time convincing people to finance your purchase of a company. Thus, your only alternative may be starting your own company.

Buying a company can be a unique experience. Although you should attempt to learn why the former management is willing to sell, it can be difficult to ascertain their reasons. When a friend of mine purchased a company, he asked the departing president why he was selling. Said the president, "I really want to try something else for a while." "Anything in particular?" my friend asked. "Yes," replied the man. "I have several things in mind, especially travel."

As things turned out, the former president used the money from the sale of the company to fly to Denmark for a sex-change operation. Six months after returning, she heard of an opening for a secretary for the company, applied for the job, and was hired because, as my friend said, she knew the most about the company, even more than the new president. The woman still works for the firm today.

Number 21 *The sixth major decision in considering forming a new company is to decide whether to use your own money, look for private financing, or try to obtain public financing.* If you use your own money, you can control your own destiny and make all the decisions. From the point of view of control, your situation is a dictator's dream. However, you will probably have to be happy with a smaller company and a slower growth rate.

Pyramid's founders did not have enough funds to go it alone, nor were there enough wealthy Egyptians willing to finance the project privately. Therefore, the company was publicly financed by the King.

Number 22 *Obtaining private financing is an excellent way of financing a company since up to 25 investors can put money into a firm without your having to register the stock with the Securities and Exchange Commission.* As long as you file the proper documents with the Commissioner of Corporations and qualify as sophisticated investors, you should be able to work within the letter of the law without too many difficulties and without preparing detailed reports. To find out what state laws affect you, you will have to check with a local lawyer.

The Egyptian government would have let Pyramid obtain private financing if enough had been available. However, it was not.

Number 23 *If you decide to seek public financing, you should be aware that four to five months will probably be needed to obtain sufficient funds and that if the stock is placed with a brokerage house, it will receive approximately a 15% commission on any money it raises.*

Ramses and Ramses, the local brokerage firm, expressed an interest, but business is good for them in gold stocks and they wanted 20%. We don't think they would spend the proper time on our deal.

Number 24 *Starting a company is never an exact process.* The founder of every company must realize that he or she is a trailblazer and expect the decision process and the financing to take as long as six to nine months.

Convincing the King to finance pyramids was a long process, involving a series of state dinners, formal audiences, and hunting outings.

Number 25 *If possible, a would-be entrepreneur should look for an expanding industry in which a small company can fight for a*

Exhibit 1

NEW COMPANY DECISION POINTS

#1	#2	#3	#4
To offer a product or a service →	For industrial use or consumer use →	To operate as a retailer or wholesaler or manufacturer →	To sell locally or regionally or nationally ↑

#5	#6
To buy a company or start a company →	To retain ownership or obtain private financing or obtain public financing

percentage of a growing market. In a static or stable industry, a small company may have a difficult time taking business away from older, established companies.

The Egyptian and world population was growing in 3000 B.C. Religion was also on the rise, and other countries would probably be raising monuments to their gods. (Besides that, King Ramses needed a classy place to be buried.)

Number 26 *The company founder should build on his or her skills, interests, and experience in starting a venture.*

King Ramses built sand castles on the banks of the Nile in his childhood.

Number 27 *Since businesses are seasonal to some extent, a company must plan on having a hedge against occasional drops in sales.*

Religious holidays will throw off Pyramid's construction schedule. It doesn't want any cut boulders piling up during the holiday period.

Number 28 *The founders of a new company can look forward to a great deal of hard work once operations have begun.* They will undoubtedly need a sense of humor in the first few weeks, particularly when what originally looked like an outstanding idea turns out to need several major modifications before it becomes workable.

Do You Have a Managerial Personality?

There is almost universal agreement that the success of any business hinges greatly on the company's management. This is especially true where tremendous growth occurs. All small businesses have some expectations of growth, and quality management is, therefore, very important.

Before embarking on a new business, it is wise to determine whether you will enjoy making the sacrifices involved. Studies have shown a variety of factors to be associated with successful entrepreneurs. Among these factors are a willingness to accept moderate risks, a position of having been a firstborn or an only child, and a history of participation in money-making ventures.

Obviously, there are successful entrepreneurs who do not match this profile. Nevertheless, those who start successful businesses do tend to have various traits in common. Primarily, most of them have:

- a strong sense of urgency about getting things done
- an inquiring mind that causes them to look at situations in a variety of ways
- an interest in the future of various markets
- confidence
- practical decision-making ability
- an ability to sell themselves and their products
- an ability to concentrate strongly on important issues

Don't be discouraged if you don't have all these characteristics. However, your chances of success in running your own business are certainly greater if you have at least some of them.

The point of the list above is to get you thinking about what type of person you really are and whether the rigors of starting a new venture fit your interests and needs. As those of us who have been through the process will attest, it's much easier to decide a new business is not for you at the *beginning* rather than halfway down the road when you have investors, employees, and customers. On the other hand, once you decide you are an individual who would enjoy and do well at this type of adventure, you can go on developing your ideas for a new business with confidence.

two

Financing a new business

*"If you would know the value of money, go
and try to borrow some."*

Benjamin Franklin

In this chapter, our mythical company, Iceberg Detectors, Inc.,
is a 1910 firm considering selling iceberg detectors for ships,
particularly passenger liners like the new Titanic.

Number 29 *Prepare a written business plan before seeking to
raise money for a new business.* A business plan can be very
brief or very lengthy, but it should be ready for potential
investors before you begin looking for funds. Several excellent
articles on developing a business plan are contained in books
offered by the most professional source of venture capital
information, Capital Publishing Company. While these books
are a bit expensive, some of the articles on the business plan
are truly excellent, and full of practical and worthwhile tips.
For information write:

Stan Pratt
Capital Publishing Co.
2 Laurel Street
Wellesley Hills, Mass.
Phone: 617-235-5405

An excellent source of information on business plans is the *Entrepreneur's Handbook,* a two-volume reference work containing some of the best articles on business plans (and other subjects of interest to entrepreneurs) ever written. To obtain a copy, write to:

Artech House
610 Washington Street
Dedham, MA 02026
Phone: (617) 326-8220

or

The Center for Entrepreneurial Management
311 Main Street
Worcester, MA 01608
Phone: (617) 755-0770

The Small Business Administration also offers several excellent pamphlets on writing a business plan:

1. The Small Marketeer Aid #153 (a business plan for small service firms); 24 pages
2. Small Marketeer Aid #150 (a business plan for retailers); 24 pages
3. Management Aid for Small Manufactures #218 (a business plan for small manufactures); 22 pages

These and other SBA pamphlets can be obtained by filling out SBA Form 115A (a list of SBA publications). Form 115A can be obtained by writing to:

The Small Business Administration
Box 15434
Fort Worth, TX 76119

Forms can also be obtained by calling, toll free, the following numbers:

  □ in Texas (800) 792-8901
  □ in other states (800) 433-7272

Yet another helpful publication is Joseph Mancuso's *How to Start, Finance, and Manage Your Own Small Business,* published by Prentice-Hall in 1977 and available in either hard or soft cover editions. The price of the soft cover edition is $8.95; that of the hard cover is $15.95. One half the book is dedicated to business plans, and there are five sample plans with commentaries in the appendix. The book may be ordered from:

> Prentice Hall
> Englewood Cliffs, NJ
> 07632

or

> The Center for Entrepreneurial Management, Inc.
> 311 Main Street
> Worcester, MA 01608

Iceberg Detector's written business plan highlights the number and type of ships regularly making Atlantic crossings and the cost of developing iceberg detectors.

Number 30 *The following outline may be useful in developing your business plan:*

1. Summary
2. Industry
3. What we propose to accomplish
4. Marketing plan
5. Production plan
6. Financial plan
7. Conclusion
8. Appendix
   a. Marketing data
   b. Cash flow estimates
   c. Balance sheet

    d. Income statement
    e. Résumés of company managers

Iceberg Detectors, Inc. proposed to sell its iceberg detectors to the U.S. and British War Departments (since the Department of the Navy didn't exist in 1910). Trials would be conducted with three ships, including the Titanic.

Number 31 *Review other companies' business plans to get ideas for preparing your own.* Business plans range from the very technical to the very simple. Some have just brief product descriptions, while others contain detailed information. A few have five words per page, plus pictures; others, especially the more technical business ones, have 500 words per page and over a hundred pages.

Iceberg Detectors, Inc. has studied the Monitor and Merrimack business plans written by the Armament Conversion Companies.

Number 32 *Ask stockbrokers, investment companies, and investors active in small business for sample business plans.* The quickest way to get a business plan is to drop in at a brokerage firm and get one of the prospectuses they offer. This will give you an idea of how to proceed.

In 1910, J. P. Morgan and Company might be able to provide a sample business plan for Ocean Crossings, Inc.

Number 33 *Even though you are not sure exactly how your company will work, get your ideas down on paper. (You'll be surprised at what ideas you develop when you do sit down to write a business plan.)* Of course, your first draft of a business plan may well be the worst thing you've ever written. Don't be discouraged. After several rewrites, you will come up with a usable summary.

Iceberg Detector's first business plan left out any mention

of the Titanic, a new ship said to have the best and newest equipment of all types. It was included as a probable customer in subsequent plans.

Number 34 *Use sample cash flow statements, income statements, and balance sheets to prepare the statements in your business plan.* Several examples of each are given in the appendix to this book. The Center for Entrepreneurial Management also offers an excellent essay on business statements called, "How to Prepare and Use Cash Flow Projections and Budgets."

Iceberg detectors are expensive and their sale will provide large cash flows. Iceberg Detector's financial statements are, therefore, very detailed.

Number 35 *Have several independent business people review your financial statements.* They will be able to spot-check your approach and offer constructive criticism. Obviously, whatever they say should be taken under advisement, but you should not guarantee that the changes they suggest will always be made. After all, it's your company, and unless you're comfortable with the changes suggested, you should stay with your original program.

Iceberg Detectors, Inc. asked a local harness manufacturer to review its business plan. He saw the market as limited to U.S. and British ships only, because of the cost.

Number 36 *The founders of a new company must consider what value they will bring to the company for stock valuation purposes and also as a negotiating point in raising funds.* If the founders are not planning to contribute funds to the company, they should review all their ideas, contracts, and production arrangements to improve their bargaining position with potential investors. Obviously, if a potential investor sees that he or she is to put up all the cash and that you, as the new company's founder-manager, are not bringing any valuable ideas or product information to the company, there is going to be trouble. At the very least, the investor is likely to demand ownership of a major portion of the company. *You should have several new product ideas that will establish your value to the company.*

Iceberg management's prior iceberg detection work, suppliers' contacts, and product designs will help all in valuing their contribution to the company.

Number 37 *You should explore with your attorneys the possibility of starting the company several months before you actually go out to raise capital.* By starting the company earlier, it will have a certain value before you attempt to raise funds. This will increase the value of your contribution to the company, since you can then say that you and your associates have spent several months developing the company.

Iceberg Detectors Incorporated was formed several months prior to requests for capital.

Number 38 *Your family and friends are usually the best initial source of investment contacts.* In some cases, they may themselves be willing to invest in the company. Or, they may know some wealthy individuals who will be willing to risk money on a new company. After receiving the names of prospective investors, call them to set up a meeting or luncheon. After the luncheon, go back to the person who provided the referral and tell him or her how things went.

None of Iceberg's founders' families could provide money for the venture, but several gave investment leads.

Number 39 *It is usually possible, and helpful, to categorize the types of private investor you are likely to encounter.* This will allow you to anticipate the types of questions particular investors will ask and the way they will react to your business plan. Do not, however, make your categories too rigid.

In 1910, there were numerous veterans of the Spanish-American War interested in Iceberg's venture.

Number 40 *One type of investor you may encounter is the Type A investor, what we call a sophisticated investor.* He (or she) will study your business plan in detail and ask a variety of questions on the direction the business will take. He also will be, if he invests, a more active participant in the company than other types of investors. For example, if he is a retired military man, he may assist you in reaching military markets and post exchanges.

Harry Kallbert, a veteran of both the Civil War and the Spanish-American War, was very interested in investing in Iceberg.

Number 41 *In talking with a sophisticated investor, be prepared to answer the question "Who else has signed up with you?"* Often, investors are like sheep. They don't want to be first to contribute to a new venture, but if others invest before them, they will gladly follow without asking too many questions. There is a large amount of herd instinct involved in investing in small companies. If several investors have already agreed to become stockholders, be quick to point this out. It may save you time in negotiating with other people. Most investors figure that there is safety in numbers. Furthermore, no one wants to be the only investor in a company that fails.

Iceberg had little trouble in attracting several investors, but several others said the product would take too long to perfect.

Number 42 *A second type of investor you will probably run into, Type B, is the technologically oriented investor.* Usually, this kind of investor has at some time or other been involved in a very technical company, either directly or indirectly. He (or she) is used to spectacularly rising or falling companies. To

appeal to him, you will have to promise that he will earn three
to five times his money in three years and ten times his
money in five years. He is used to investing in technical
products that either find a large market very quickly or die
quickly. It is very difficult to sell this type of investor on a
slow-growing company that will develop a solid market over
a period of ten or fifteen years. He is usually looking for quick
action.

One technologically oriented investor told Iceberg that it
needed to modify its product further. He believed it would
not be available for the maiden voyage of the Titanic.

Number 43 *In dealing with a technologically oriented investor,
you will get numerous questions regarding patents.* You should
be prepared to say whether it will be possible to patent any
of your products or services and what approach you will take
in seeking patents. You should also expect very heavy questioning about the strength of your product line. Offering a
service will not usually appeal to this type of investor, and
your product line must be broad enough, technical enough,
and different enough to have a *competitive advantage.* It is
very difficult to make a marketing company attractive to a
technologically oriented investor who is primarily looking for
a new product.

Iceberg's detector was definitely patentable, but the firm
was not sure how the patent office would test the product.

Number 44 *In talking to a technologically oriented investor, you
should stress all the technical advantages of your product and how
it compares with competing products.* New companies with
detailed technology are among the easiest to finance, especially in the San Francisco Bay peninsula or around Route 128
in Boston.

Iceberg had no competitors, since its product was new.

Number 45 *If you have a high-technology product, it may be very helpful for you to have a technological advisor or a board of directors with technical backgrounds.* Perhaps a professor from a local college may be willing to act as an advisor. Harold Williams, a Professor of Physics at Eastern University, was a charter member of Iceberg's board of directors.

Number 46 *A third type of potential investor, Type C, is the job-seeker.* Unless you are willing to take unusual risks, this type of investor should be avoided. Normally, you can identify job-seekers by asking them directly whether, if they were to invest in the company, they would want a position with it. The problem with job-seekers as investors is that the money they invest primarily goes back to them as salaries. Usually, the founders of a company are barely in a position to pay themselves a salary at the beginning, let alone anyone else! Several job-seeking investors have approached Iceberg. Since they had no specialized knowledge of iceberg detectors, no positions were offered them.

Number 47 *If an entrepreneur is starting a new company alone and can gain specialized knowledge from a job-seeking investor, it may be worthwhile to have the job-seeker in the company. If not, the job-seeker should be avoided.* In Iceberg's case, it is planned to avoid all job-seeking investors.

Venture-Capital Firms

Number 48 *Always consider venture-capital firms as a source of financing for a small business.* Venture capitalists specialize in high-risk investments and are very familiar with a variety of business plans. They negotiate very tough deals with new companies, but are a potential source of capital.

Turn-of-the-Century Venture Capital, a New York firm, helped Iceberg Detectors get off the ground.

Number 49 *In dealing with venture-capital firms, try to avoid being screened by lower-echelon employees. If possible, secure an appointment with a partner or an officer of the firm.* Venture-capital firms look at a variety of investments every week, and unless your ideas are extraordinarily unique, it's difficult to get them interested in you.

Theodore Harris, a senior partner in a 1910 venture-capital firm, said "Iceberg detectors have a great future."

Other Sources of Investment Capital

Number 50 *Ask each potential investor you talk with to recommend other likely investors.* Often an individual who knows various wealthy people will screen prospective investments for them. Although such a person will expect a fee, for helping you, it is well worth paying if it saves you time.

Charles Comstock, a local New York financier, helped Iceberg attract several investors. His fee was high, but he earned it.

Number 51 *Stockbrokers are frequent sources of investors for new companies.* There are restrictions on how stockbrokers invest the funds of their accounts. Often, however, they will know people who do not wish to invest all their funds in the stock or bond market and would be willing to invest in a small company. Why would a stockbroker be willing to do this when he or she receives no commission on such a deal? The main reason is to impress investors with the range of contacts the broker has. There is a certain personal reward in being able to tell clients that several investors are putting some money into a small company that is just getting started. Iceberg's third-largest investor, A. J. Harris, was introduced to the firm by her broker.

Number 52 *A financial finder can be very helpful, particularly one who will work on a commission basis.* One man we're familiar with who does this, was a banker for ten years. He knows how to evaluate small companies. He also has numerous contacts in the community and knows the current officers of two banks personally.

Financial finders will always ask to see the company's business plan and may suggest several revisions. You obviously should consider their suggestions. The way some deals are structured will depend on the finder's commitments to the arrangement and his or her ability to sell friends and potential accounts. Do not rewrite your business plan simply to satisfy a financial finder, but do consider some changes to make the plan more marketable as long as they do not run counter to your own business philosophy and goals.

Wesley Harriman, a finder for Iceberg, worked on a commission basis and did not charge the firm unless he actually raised funds for it.

Number 53 *Unless all other avenues of investment have been exhausted, do not, we repeat, do not, rely on an investment finder who demands a retainer.* Most of these people ask retainers ranging from $200 to $2,000 per month. If they manage to bring some funds into the company, their fees are normally subtracted from this money. However, if you work with a financial finder for $2,000 a month for six months and he is unable to bring in any funds to the company, you are out $12,000. In 1910, the going rate for finders who worked on a retainer basis was $400 per month.

Number 54 *It is unlikely that a financial finder will accept stock in a company in lieu of a finder's fee (normally 10%) or a retainer fee.* The finder will always argue, as a friend of ours does, that he has his own expenses to pay and that it may be more than three years before the stock in the company is worth something. He is being charitable. He knows all too well the odds are against a new company surviving for long in today's competitive business environment.

Iceberg was never in this position.

Number 55 *Occasionally, in large cities, you will meet attorneys who act as informal advisors, but who receive fees only for filing incorporation papers and doing other legal work for a new company.* If you can find such an individual, by all means try to work with him (or her). This is a very low-cost way of finding investors. Obviously, you are under no legal requirement to use an attorney's services simply because he has introduced you to certain investors. However, he will normally expect to handle some of your legal business.

Hiram Harris, a New York attorney, was helping Iceberg attract investors.

Number 56 *You should not waste your time working with licensed investment advisors in seeking financing for a new company.* These individuals work for an annual fee of 1% of the funds they manage, and often supervise the investments of wealthy families. Since they receive a flat fee each year, they have the flexibility to invest in any kind of undertaking. They usually have cash available and might be willing, you would think, to take a flyer with a small company.

Unfortunately for the would-be entrepreneur, most investment advisors are very conservative and are not interested in committing funds to new companies. They feel that they are managing family funds and that it is up to them to seek secure investments. Several new rules regarding the licensing and operations of independent investment advisors have also caused them to restrict the type of investments they will consider. Primarily, they stick to stocks and bonds, real estate, or savings accounts.

In 1910, Walker Robinson, a licensed investment advisor managing funds for many wealthy families, turned down Iceberg's request for an interview.

Number 57 *Investors, like other sophisticated buyers, have to be sold through frequent discussions.* While there are many stories about investors who agree immediately to invest in a struggling new company, such tales, in our experience, have little basis in reality. Creative selling and hard work are what brings results! Many investors appreciate the fact that you will go to a variety of lengths to make sure that all their questions are answered. They feel that you will work equally hard to make your company a success.

After 12 meetings with Iceberg, Wesley Cummins, an associate of John D. Rockefeller, agreed to invest $30,000 (a princely sum in 1910) into the company.

Number 58 *Beware of statements such as "Well, I'm thinking of putting my money in. . . . "* No investor can be considered definitely committed to a company until he or she has signed an agreement to that effect. Until then, you should not assume that the investor is truly willing to sign and you should keep up your campaign to get him or her "on board."

Fortunately for Iceberg, none of its investors backed out of verbal commitments to supply funds.

Number 59 *The effect of taxes should always be considered in preparing to talk with potential investors.* If investors are able to write off half of their investment, they are more likely to risk their funds on a new company. Investors in the 50% bracket are not likely to be overly concerned if the company doesn't survive, and therefore, tend to be the best kind of investors to have. The worst kind of investor is someone living on a limited income who wishes to put money in "a sure thing."

Number 60 *Of course, if a small company does fail, the founders can still offer their stockholders one benefit—provided their lawyers were on the ball in the beginning and took advantage of Section 1244 of the Internal Revenue Code.* This section, established to encourage investments in small business, gives stockholders the right to write off against ordinary income up to $50,000 due to the failure of the company during any tax year. The $50,000 ceiling is for a joint return, even if you and your spouse separately owned stock. For an individual return, the limit is $25,000. If the loss is sustained by a partnership, the $25,000 or $50,000 limit on write-offs, is determined separately for each partner.

The ordinary loss deduction is treated as a business loss— it can be carried back three years and forward seven years. Any loss over the $25,000 (or $50,000) limit comes under the less favorable rules for capital losses, unless it can be spread over more than one year.

For example, assume a married person invests $200,000 in a business that proves unsuccessful and can unload the stock for only $40,000. If he sells half of it for $20,000 this year and half the next year for the same price, he can take an ordinary write-off of $50,000 each year—a total of $100,000.

Qualifying stockholders for this special break merely requires including certain language in the corporate minutes when the stock is first issued. Since there is nothing to lose and everything to gain, every "small business corporation" should automatically do this.

A Subchapter Selection allows a corporation to pass operating losses directly through to its shareholders so that they can deduct them on their personal tax returns. But even for a Subchapter S corporation, it is useful to qualify under Section

1244. Going that route permits shareholders to treat as an ordinary loss a drop in value *greater than the operating losses passed through.* If no Section 1244 plan has been adopted, only $3,000 of a net capital loss can be used to offset ordinary income.

Since income taxes were of little moment in 1910, Iceberg did not concern itself with such matters.

Number 61 *You should not lose any sleep at night wondering if investors in the company will suddenly discover, after six months or so, that they need their money back.* Every investor in a small company should be considered an adult who understands the risks involved. Worrying about such things is a waste of energy.

In order to manufacture its product, Iceberg needed, and obtained, a long-term financial commitment from its investors.

Number 62 *Even for those who support the Protestant work ethic, there is an enormous amount of work involved in trying to get financing for a small company.* You should expect as many as five to seven meetings with each potential investor in your company before a deal is finally made and signed. It is best to keep a sense of humor throughout this process and not assume that any of the horses are in the barn until the doors have been shut and locked.

Even though Iceberg was to be a relatively small company, financing took over a year to find.

three

Dealing with banks and investors

"A banker is a man who lends you an umbrella when the weather is fair and takes it away from you when it rains."

Anonymous

In this chapter, we discuss financing a company, Shark Repellent, Inc., that plans to produce a shark repellent for ocean swimmers and divers.

Getting Financing from Banks

Number 63 *During the start-up phase of your company, consider approaching a bank directly for a loan.* Most people starting a small company have not had much to do with banks, except as depositors or holders of personal checking accounts. It is very helpful, however, to know something about the process by which one secures a business loan from a bank and the long-term benefits of being able to repay the loan. Having a bank loan will eventually establish a new company as a good credit risk and help in its development.

Shark Repellent, Inc., a West Coast company, approached the Bank of America, the world's largest bank, for a loan.

Number 64 *Ask your friends if they know of a banker who concentrates on small businesses.* Often an attorney, an insurance broker, or the owner of a small business will know of a friendly banker with whom you should talk. Repellent's attorney recommended that it talk to Walker Harris, a Bank of America loan officer experienced in dealing with small companies.

Number 65 *Stockholders and directors of other newly formed small companies are excellent sources of capital and leads for bank funds.* Several investors in Shark Repellent, Inc. provided names of recently financed West Coast companies and their directors. Repellent's officers followed up on these leads.

Number 66 *Always consider recent positive economic news in discussing a potential new company with a banker.* The Federal Reserve Bank issues statements every three months about the business climate for the next year. These statements are a valuable way of verifying how advantageous a time it is to start a new company.

News of expected low unemployment rates, stable interest rates, and higher corporate profits convinced the president of Shark Repellent, Inc. to push harder for a bank loan.

Number 67 *All bankers, in reviewing loan applications, calculate how soon the loan can be repaid.* The auditors who review bank loans feel that banks should not be locked into long-term corporate investments and, therefore, should not provide permanent capital for small companies. For this reason, most loan officers will review your cash-flow statements and calculate with a view to determining how soon the bank can be repaid.

They will say to you, for example, "We would like to have your $60,000 loan completely paid off for one month a year." This is a standard procedure, called being "out of the bank" for a period of time. Because banks like to operate this way, you may have to settle for a slower rate of growth than if you used other sources of financing. Often, instead of using money from your customers for new inventory or tooling, you will have to use it to repay the bank. Banks always specify that they are to be paid first. As a rule, the best course is to include in your cash-flow statement a line showing how soon a loan will be repaid.

Repellent and its banker, estimated that if all went reasonably well, the bank would be repaid gradually over three years and the company would be out of the bank every December through February.

Number 68 *In seeking bank financing for a new venture, don't overlook the value of the SBA as a guarantor of loans.* The SBA seldom lends money directly to a new venture, but it often guarantees bank loans to help firms secure financing. The SBA is most helpful in securing loans for companies that are marginal credit risks. An SBA guarantee of a bank loan can result in:

1. a longer term for the loan (up to 7 years),
2. a lower interest rate (since the SBA sets the bank rate), and
3. a little more money (since banks like SBA guarantees).

The major drawback of an SBA-guaranteed loan is that the entrepreneur will have to pledge his or her personal assets as support for the loan.

Line 23 on the company's cash-flow statement shows that if sales of the shark repellent lotion ("Hands Off") are good, the company will be out of the bank every December through February.

Number 69 *Don't figure that your investors will lend you additional money so that you can be out of the bank for one month a* *year.* Most large private investors have substantial assets. However, much of their capital may be tied up in real estate, which takes time to convert into cash. Shark Repellent, Inc. did not need to request any additional loans from stockholders.

Number 70 *A new company must give as much warning to its investors as possible if repayment of bank loans or requests for new financing are being considered.* As we discussed above, investors generally need time to generate money to repay bank loans or contribute additional capital to a company.

Shark Repellent, Inc. expects no need for further funds unless its principal product, "Hands Off Lotion" fails to sell as expected.

Number 71 *Most banks expect you to revolve their loans.* You will need to make periodic payments on a bank loan and then sign forms to receive additional funds up to your credit limit. This procedure shows that the bank financing is not permanent capital and that the company can make periodic payments. Your repayments will depend on how well the business does and its need for cash.

Number 72 *The most important question any banker will ask is how much equity capital has been put into the company.* Banks normally prefer a firm to have a maximum debt-to-equity ratio of one. In other words, if there is only $30,000 in paid-in capital, the bank will make only a $30,000 loan.

Shark Repellent, Inc. has raised $200,000 in capital and preliminary discussions indicated that the Bank of America was willing to match that amount.

Number 73 *99% of bank loans to companies are made by a business loan committee.* It is important, therefore, to give the lending officer enough information to make a presentation to the committee. The loan officer alone will not make the final decision.

Shark Repellent's president discussed its loan application with each member of the bank's loan committee.

Number 74 *With a small company, expect that a bank loan will have to be guaranteed by the investors in the company or by the management.* In other words, the bank will require the investors in the company to guarantee in writing to repay the loan if anything happens to the company.

Shark Repellent's investors fully expected to guarantee its loan.

Number 75 *New company managers should ask their investors to guarantee bank loans, but should avoid signing anything themselves except as a last resort.* If the new company managers fail to limit their liability in this way and the company doesn't make it, they may never be able to start another company. Although the bankruptcy laws may enable managers to protect some of their assets (such as their homes), many of their assets may be lost if a firm goes under.

Shark Repellent's president did not personally guarantee the bank loan. This was wise, since he has limited personal assets.

Number 76 *You should prepare potential investors to sign a note requiring each of them separately to guarantee the entire bank loan.* Banks will usually press for this. For example, if you are getting a $60,000 loan and have six investors, all the investors will be required to guarantee the full $60,000 rather than $10,000 each.

Number 77 *You should also ask your attorney to draw up a separate agreement guaranteeing your investors some recourse if one investor is unable to pick up his share of the bank loan.*

A separate agreement to this effect was drawn up by Shark Repellent's attorney Howard Fish.

Number 78 *It is very helpful for the founder of a new company seeking a bank loan to be in telephone contact with the banker at least every two days while the loan application is being reviewed.* Loan committee members often raise several questions about a loan application during the review period. It is best to try to answer these questions as soon as possible to pave the way for a final vote on the loan.

Shark Repellent's president called his banker every day to discuss his loan application.

Number 79 *It is often effective to suggest to investors who are reluctant to guarantee bank loans or to put money into a company, that they would be better off with some of their money out of the stock market.* In many cases new investors have been sold on the idea of putting money directly into a new company instead of sitting still for stock market losses.

Shark Repellent persuaded seven of its investors to come on board in this fashion.

Number 80 *If you are turned down by four or more banks, it is time to look elsewhere for funds.* At this point, you need to rethink your approach to financing and consider increasing your equity capital.

A friend of Shark Repellent's president, after numerous turndowns, gave up on banks as a source of initial capital.

Number 81 *If a company has more than two or three investors, a legal agreement spelling out their rights and liabilities is mandatory.* Have your attorney prepare the proper documents. Next, review them in person with each potential investor. After that, review all changes with the entire group of investors by telephone. Finally, if necessary, have another individ-

ual meeting with each potential investor. Do not gather all
the investors together for a meeting. This often causes problems, as several investors demand restrictions that others will
not agree to.

A seven-page legal agreement on investors' rights and
obligations was drafted by Howard Fish, Shark Repellent's
attorney.

Number 82 *Seasonality must be considered in discussing cash
flows with bankers. Every business is seasonal.* Talking about
seasonality with potential customers is a very effective way to
estimate peaks and valleys in sales.

Discussions with swimmers and divers showed that Shark
Repellent's business would be very seasonal, with mostly
spring and summer sales.

Number 83 *If the individual with whom you have been negotiating a loan leaves his or her job for any reason, always insist on
an introduction to his or her replacement or supervisor.* Often you
will receive prompt attention from new individuals responsible for departed employees' work because they are anxious
to demonstrate their helpfulness and efficiency.

Walker Harris, Shark Repellent's banker, had shown no
inclination to leave his bank so this problem did not occur.

Number 84 *Be prepared to have the majority of bankers ask the
following question: "What makes you think all this is going to
work?"*

Shark Repellent is sure its lotion will sell because it meets
a real need effectively.

Number 85 *When you are starting a new company, it is almost
impossible to gauge how long it will take to complete financial
arrangements with a bank.* If anything, calculate at least a

month for a loan application to be reviewed. If time is on your side, allow at least two months.

Shark Repellent applied for its bank loan two months before it planned to begin production of its lotion. During the interim, the formula for the lotion was refined.

Attracting Investors

Number 86 *Always keep in mind that a potential investor is interested primarily in the return on an investment and the risk it entails.* The founder of a new company will undoubtedly encounter investors willing to talk about football, the weather, their children, their house, previous deals, or industries they have invested in. However, in the back of each investor's mind are two points: (1) If he or she puts in $5,000, what are the chances of making three, four, or five times that amount? and (2) How likely is it that funds invested in the company will be lost?

Shark Repellent estimated that its investors *could* make five times their original investment in three years. The chances were only one in five that this would occur, however.

Number 87 *A second consideration for most investors, not as important as paybacks or risks, is whether they can, if necessary, get their money out of the company, and if so, how long it will take.* You should be prepared to answer these questions.

A small businessman once told an interesting story about an investor who wanted to get his money out of one of the companies he had invested in. Six years ago, he had invested in a small food franchising business. The company started out selling cheesecake to local restaurants. An entrepreneur who had made money selling roast beef franchises found out that the company was for sale and went to a brokerage firm to raise money. One of the brokerage firm's executives was originally negative about the idea because of the extent to which the Sara Lee brand dominated the cheesecake market. However, he changed his mind and decided that the local cheesecake company was an excellent investment. As for the investor, he believed that the local cheesecake company could become a new Kentucky Fried Chicken via franchising. (Pointing to a profitable company as a model for your own often inspires investor confidence.)

Several problems soon arose. Though the firm's fresh cheesecakes sold well in local restaurants, they lasted only three or four days. This created a problem with regard to national distribution. The firm couldn't truck cheesecake from Los Angeles to New York because that would take 10 days. It couldn't air freight the fresh cheesecake because of the costs involved. To make a profit it would have to charge an exorbitant $2.00 per slice.

Because the cheesecake company didn't have the funds for a fresh cheesecake plant in each city where a franchise store was proposed, the company president looked around for another idea. Soon he was developing pie shops with a Pennsylvania Dutch decor. The shops were located in suburban shopping centers and the pies could be eaten in the store or taken home. Original Pennsylvania Dutch recipes were used and a Betty Crocker-type woman was hired to promote the pie shops.

Why is all this important? The point is that all these changes in the firm's plans and products took time and money. The investor's funds were tied up in the company for six years and he had received no dividends. It might be another five or six years before the company's investors could even begin to take their money out. Even if the company were sold, investors might have to settle for stock in the new company rather than cash.

Shark Repellent's investors all hoped that its lotion would soon become popular, thus improving the firm's cash position.

Number 88 *Occasionally, a letter stating that if a new outside investor wishes to invest in a company, that individual will be referred to any current investor interested in selling his or her stock, will be helpful in calming investor fears of being locked in.* However, you should assume that each investor understands his or her funds will be invested in the company for a minimum of three to five years.

All Shark Repellent's investors understood that their investment would be for a minimum of three years.

Number 89 *Never stop selling your company until all your investors are signed up.* Occasionally, it is very effective to make elaborate efforts to sign an investor. I have a friend who tracked one investor down by calling all the hotels in Honolulu to find out where he and his wife were staying on vacation. This tactic was effective since the investor believed that my friend would be similarly persevering in making the company a success.

All Shark Repellent's investors were systematically courted and signed.

Number 90 *It is illegal to deposit or accept funds for a new company until a permit has been approved by the Commissioner of Corporations of the state in which you are working.* The exact requirements in your state can be learned through a telephone call to the state department responsible for corporations.

Shark Repellent, Inc. complied with all California rules for doing business including obtaining a permit.

Number 91 *Avoid, at all costs, taking a promissory note from an investor in lieu of cash.* Giving a note is an excuse for not putting money into the company. Our experience has been that it is very difficult to collect seed money from an investor who insists on putting up a note instead of putting capital into a firm. This can cause tremendous problems, since cash flows from operations may not be regular, especially in the beginning. Increases in overhead also are difficult to project. If you have cash in the bank, you will have it when you need it. If you have to track down an investor and pressure him into paying on his note, you may end up with nothing.

One investor in Shark Repellent wanted to give the firm a note and promised to put up cash once the lotion was actually produced. The company president refused to agree to this.

Number 92 *Good relations with new stockholders are important.* A frequent (once-a-month) luncheon or a newsletter should be considered as a way of keeping new stockholders in touch with what's going on.

Shark Repellent, Inc. planned to have a monthly luncheon for stockholders.

Number 93 *Talking with many investors is typical in starting a new company.* Generally, a new company must discuss financing with 30 or 40 investors in order to find five or six who are really interested in putting up cash capital.

Shark Repellent cultivated over 50 investors to obtain its eight stockholders.

In this chapter, we have discussed the factors that should be considered before talking with banks and private investors. We cannot stress too often the importance of having a detailed business plan, including an estimated cash-flow statement and balance sheet before beginning your search for financing. Starting a new company is not a straight-line process. There is often a considerable amount of negotiation, changing of agreements, and discussion even if the company is to be a fairly simple one and the documentation standard.

four

The first 60 days

*"He has half the deed done who has made
the beginning."*

Horace

In this chapter, we consider the initial days in 1811 of a winter
clothing manufacturer, the Arctic Clothing Company. Arctic
hopes to supply Napoleon for his upcoming Russian campaign.

Number 94 *The person starting a new company should never
burn all his or her bridges in resigning from a previous job, since
it may be necessary to ask for the job back if things don't work
out.* The best way to leave is on friendly terms, expressing
regret at going and saying the opportunity to try your hand
at something new is too good to pass up. Pierre La Rousse,
founder of Arctic Clothing, resigned his previous job as
manager of a medium-sized garment manufacturer in a friendly discussion with his boss.

Number 94A *Running a small business sometimes requires an
unconventional approach.* When should conventional wisdom

be discarded in favor of contrary thinking? Here are four rules of unconventional wisdom:

1. When you *don't* need capital is the optimal time to raise it.
2. When your backlog of orders is high is the optimal time to call a meeting of dealers or sales representatives.
3. When shipments and bookings are high is the optimal time to advertise.
4. When many small companies are giving up and the times appear bleak can be the ideal time to think about launching a new venture.

The rationale for these rules is as follows:

1. Bank lines of credit and new equity capital should be arranged when you don't need them desperately. Human nature, being what it is, it's often easiest to get help when you're doing fine. Nobody likes a loser.
2. When sales are low, it's natural to try and raise them, but it's the wrong time to call a rah-rah sales meeting. It pulls the sales staff off the road just when you need them there, and it gives them a chance to commiserate with one another, which can be self-defeating.
3. When sales are above forecasts is the best time to advertise. The time lag between advertising and sales is usually sufficient to warrant advertising during your peak sales month. The results will be apparent a few months afterwards.
4. When interest rates are high and stock prices are low, capital tends to dry up and small companies die. This is an ideal time to think about starting a new business, as its eventual birth will then be perfectly timed to

coincide with the inevitable economic upswing that follows a recession.

Arctic Clothing used unconventional reasoning when it decided to include swimsuits in its product line. The company management felt that the soldiers might use the swimsuits as undergarments, since they were comfortable and more desirable than conventional underwear.

Number 95 *For a new company, low overhead costs are a critical factor.* Often, a new company must begin with a small support staff, such as a secretary for writing letters and typing. You can always sell inventory at a small loss, but once you spend a dollar on overhead, it is gone forever. Low overhead may help a new company survive!

For its initial headquarters, the Arctic Clothing Company chose a loft in a low-rent district just outside Paris.

Number 96 *Since a new company normally can't afford to hire salespeople, manufacturers' representatives are usually the best way of merchandising products.* Manufacturers' representatives work on commission and don't get paid unless they make a sale. They are normally in daily contact with the buyers they sell to and know what products are needed. They can assess the chances of your product making it and may be able to suggest modifications or marketing approaches you have not thought of.

The organizations listed below often help small businesses find competent sales representatives.

Robert Benham   Direct Selling Association
Representative Resources, Inc.   1730 M Street, Northwest
Drower Avenue   Suite 610
Thorndale, PA 19372   Washington, DC 20036
Phone: (215) 383-1177   Phone: (202) 293-5760

Members of this association sell products and services directly to consumers, primarily in their homes.

Manufacturers Agents National Association (MANA)
2021 Business Center Drive
Box 16878
Irvine, CA 92713

This 30-year old association of manufacturers' agents is an excellent source of information.

NEMEX
10 Moulton Street
Cambridge, MA 02138
Phone: (617) 354-1150

This New England Manufacturing Exchange (NEMEX) is a clearinghouse that maintains up-to-date computerized information on products offered by some 1,400 suppliers.

Pacific International
P. O. Box 894
Escondido, CA 92025
Phone: (714) 741-7484
President: Gordon Strickler

Pacific International maintains qualified sales representatives in 42 major marketing areas in the United States and Canada.

Skilled French manufacturer's representatives will sell Arctic Clothing's products to Napoleon's supply officers.

Number 97 *It's a good idea to ask your manufacturer's representative or a potential manufacturer's representative to suggest improvements in your product or service.*

Arctic Clothing's representatives stressed the severity of the Russian winter and suggested extra padding in all garments.

Number 98 *Remember that, in a growing industry, just about any product that is an improvement on existing products will be* *salable.* In a slowly growing industry, there is often such a large inventory of existing products in marketing channels, stores, and warehouses that it is very difficult to get a new product introduced and established. In an industry that is growing rapidly and has a high turnover rate for inventory, your product is likely to get to the stores quickly if it has any advantages at all.

Arctic Clothing expected little problem in marketing its products since Napoleon's army was famous for its rapid growth.

Number 99 *Sometimes a new company finds it necessary to come up with a product it can sell for a short period, even though it*

knows sales will not continue over a number of years. The obvious reason for this is to try to generate some cash to pay part of the company's overhead during the initial months. Arctic Clothing expected to sell fall jackets to people around Paris until it geared up to produce heavier winter clothing.

Number 100 *To stimulate sales, consider combination products with multiple uses.* For example, a nylon pack that could be used as a bicycle saddle bag worked well for one manufacturer. Carryalls for both tennis gear and tennis rackets are also popular. Often, a manufacturer's representative can suggest combination products that would be salable in the marketplace.

One of Arctic's first products was designed to serve as both a winter jacket and a lining for sleeping bags.

Number 101 *Never promise a manufacturers' representative a product that's only on the drawing board.* Otherwise, he or she may be constantly pressuring you about it. Wait till you've got a production schedule to set a delivery date, and then stick to that date. Missing it will not generate confidence in your representative.

Arctic Clothing was very reluctant to promise any products in time for the fast-approaching winter. It felt Napoleon might do well to delay his campaign a year until the army could be better clothed.

Number 102 *In some industries, it is very valuable to talk to a potential manufacturers' representative before going into production.* The discussion may turn up several facts that will help you in setting up production schedules. For example, one company, in talking to a manufacturers' representative, learned that a competitor was so slow in making deliveries that stores were cancelling their orders. The new company quickly filled this void.

Arctic's representatives were very helpful in helping it design clothing suitable for both footsoldiers and cavalry.

Number 103 *A new company should always add two to four weeks to its most conservative estimate of product availability.* It is very important for a new company to do what it says it will do and deliver products on time. Schedules should be met even if it means working evenings or beefing up a production force. Once a new company misses delivery dates, customers lose confidence in it.

Number 104 *Be very careful about making long-range marketing commitments.* You may wish to do things differently in six months. Do not let yourself be locked into a long-term agreement with a particular manufacturers' representative. Even he or she may wish to do something else in six months.

Initially, Arctic did not hire any permanent sales representatives.

Number 105 *If you are the sole founder of a new company, it's best to train someone else, possibly your spouse, to run the company in your absence.* It is important to have somebody who, if he or she cannot entirely replace you, can at least keep the company going in the critical first months if you become sick or find it necessary to be out of town.

Pierre La Rousse, Arctic's president, had his wife supervise his workforce. She learned a good deal about the business and could take over if he was absent.

Number 106 *Always look for a manufacturers' representative who has at least one well-known product line.* That well-known line will often get him or her into the store to sell your products. For example, if you were planning to sell ski-wear and your representative also sold a popular brand of skis, he would probably be very valuable to you.

Arctic's representatives also marketed Le Clip, a silver horse spur widely used by the military.

Number 107 *Plan for a period of slow growth for your company.* Patience is one of the most important attributes of successful entrepreneurs.

Arctic wasn't sure it could produce enough winter clothing for Napoleon's army the first year, but it was certain that the Russian campaign would take two years. Of course, by the second year, competitors were likely to arise too.

Number 108 *Attending trade shows of overseas suppliers is an excellent way of determining what products are being offered in an industry and also of establishing production contacts overseas.* Trading companies in many overseas countries will make all arrangements for manufacturing merchandise and shipping it to the United States. It is possible to send the trading company a sample of your product and receive production quotes in return. The most obvious advantage of overseas production is lower labor costs.

Arctic considered using newly discovered French colonies to make clothing. However, shipping delays were common and winter clothing arriving in summer would be disastrous.

Number 109 *Consider U.S. production for low-labor-content products and overseas production for high-labor-content products.* While patriotism may dictate that you make all your products in the United States, if you wish your company to survive, it may be necessary to consider overseas production. At the moment, Japan, Taiwan, India, and Singapore seem to be the best places for making products overseas. For clothing, Hong

Kong can be a good place. U.S. labor can't compete with many
wage rates overseas. In Korea, for example, $3.00 a day, or
30¢ an hour, is apparently enough to sustain a family of four.
But a new company can sometimes redesign its product or
mechanize its production enough to lower the amount of labor
in the total cost of the product.

Arctic was able to price its clothing reasonably while still
using domestic labor.

Number 110 *In considering overseas production, remember that
foreign products are frequently not of the same quality as U.S.
products.* Production facilities overseas are often rudimentary,
and extreme care is needed to ensure the quality you wish in
a product. For a long time, semiconductor manufacturers had
to throw out about half the semiconductor parts they received
from Taiwan. Because of labor costs, this was still cheaper
than manufacturing the parts in the United States.

Since French clothing products were of excellent quality,
Arctic expected no competition from overseas firms.

Number 111 *It helps a new company to be on overseas mailing
lists.* If nothing else, it keeps you current about new products.
Taiwan, for example, publishes a monthly magazine that is a
valuable resource. Of course, numerous people receive these
magazines, so to be truly innovative, you should go beyond
the products offered in them. Attending a foreign trade show
is an excellent way to survey products being made overseas
and to avoid costly production mistakes. Several stories have
been told about companies that designed a new product,
looked around the United States, and found out that they
could make the product better and more cheaply than anyone
in the country. They then went out and spent tens of thou-
sands of dollars to produce the product, only to find out that

someone in Japan or Taiwan was making it at a much lower cost.

Arctic Clothing had contacts in the New World and the Orient that kept it aware of most new production processes.

Number 112 *Select a low-rent office.* A low-rent office is very important in keeping the overhead of a new company down. Inexpensive quarters not only give investors the idea that you are doing your best to conserve their capital, but also help you present a restrained image to banks and future suppliers. Our personal experience has been that having a very high-priced, statusy office actually raises suspicions on the part of bankers, investors, and potential suppliers as to whether you will be able to pay your bills.

For a new company, sharing office space is often an effective way to lower costs. It also provides contact with other people during the day if you're going it alone. As for furnishings, you can often find secondhand furniture at a discount office-supply outlet. With about $500 and some secondhand desks, you can furnish an office for three or four people. This sets a frugal tone for the entire company that is often helpful. It's difficult to demand economy from others while you're sitting behind a $1,000 desk.

Arctic furnished its low-cost loft quarters with several workbenches and desks made by a local carpenter.

Number 113 *Never purchase half-developed or half-finished projects.* There are numerous companies and individuals around who are more than willing to sell you a product that has been developed "to a certain stage." However, what generally happens is that the investors either run out of money or find out that the product is not as salable as they originally thought. Often the individual developing the product has made a number of early mistakes that were costly and is trying to recoup some of his or her investment.

Several local outfits have offered Arctic half-finished designs for clothing, but none appeared suitable for military use.

Number 114 *A new company should stick to its basic approach and should never buy a product package or service product that is unfamiliar to the company's managers.* Very simply, if you are in the tennis business, you should not be buying ideas for new bicycles unless you are also very familiar with the bicycle business.

All Arctic's officers understood the clothing business. None were interested in going into any other businesses as sidelines.

Number 115 *The proprietor of a new company should thoroughly study the cost of completing a new product project without assistance.* Instead of buying a completed product or a half-completed product from someone else, you should start from scratch and make improvements to the product by developing it yourself.

Arctic developed its clothing designs entirely by itself.

Number 116 *Always read industry publications related to your company's business.* If you can't afford to purchase these publications because they are expensive, you can always go to the nearest business library. In most cases, you will find the publications you are looking for there. One West Coast company used industry publications to find suppliers of components for a new product it was developing.

No regular publications on the clothing industry were available to Arctic, but it did read various government reports on the military.

Number 117 *In dealing with potential overseas suppliers, it is imperative to give estimated quantities.* Any overseas company worth its salt will not touch a small project (less than 10,000 units) unless the long-term prospect is good. To interest an overseas supplier in making your product, you will probably have to promise verbally that if the product sells well, there will be a substantial volume of business for the supplier.

Since all Arctic's manufacturing was to be done domestically, it didn't have this problem.

Number 118 *During the initial phases of a new company, investigate subcontracting your production work.* It's pretty silly to lease a 30,000-square-foot plant and buy $100,000 worth of equipment only to find out that a product won't sell or that you can't produce it at a low enough cost. Instead consider whether the production operation could be subcontracted to a firm in the area already doing similar work. Most people fear, when considering this alternative, that the production company will steal the product and market it themselves. The solution may be a short written agreement with the production company in which it agrees not to market the product, design a competing version of it, or compete in any other way. Normally, the production company will be happy to make your product if they have any excess capacity. In fact, they may need you as much as you need them.

Almost all Arctic's knitting will be subcontracted to Paris seamstresses. They will complete the work in their homes.

Number 119 *Whenever you subcontract a production operation, insist on seeing actual machinery that will be used or the workplaces where your product will be made.* One trick a production company can use is to farm out your work to someone else in the area. It is always important to deal directly with the plant or company that will produce the product so that you can get it for the lowest cost possible.

In Arctic Clothing's case, the president's wife visited most of the homes where the clothing was to be made.

Number 120 *Always allow an additional two weeks for the first units of any product you plan to produce to come off the assembly line.* It generally takes at least three months to get all the kinks out of a new product. If it's a highly technological product, three years may be a more likely average. Often, however, an entrepreneur will have worked on a product and completed much of its development before starting a company to produce it. If this is the case, an attempt may be made to introduce the product early.

Arctic planned to give itself ample time to produce enough clothing to equip the army. However, it knew that if Napoleon marched sooner than expected, it would have to pressure its seamstresses to work faster.

Number 121 *Having a balance of easy-to-produce and difficult-to-produce products is a very effective hedge against product failure.* There may be several easy-to-produce products for which you can get a piece of the market. Including them in your product line may save your neck if problems arise in manufacturing more complicated items. It may also allow you to make more use of your production capacity and your sales representatives.

Arctic planned to produce bedrolls and blankets for the soldiers, as well as capes, jackets, and leggings.

Number 122 *Actual visits to purchase merchandise are mandatory.* Always see for yourself what merchandise is available and check what you will be receiving. A personal visit to your suppliers will show them that you care what they send you and are a careful businessperson.

Pierre La Rousse visited many sheep farms in southern France to check the quality of their wool.

Number 123 *Always set up a bookkeeping system right away.* If you can't afford a bookkeeper or an accountant, do the book-keeping yourself. Set up a simple system for listing the checks that are written and those that come in. A library book on accounting will tell you what accounts to set up. For example, you probably should have separate accounts for advertising, postage, salaries, state taxes, federal taxes, rent, office ex-penses, and supplies.

The Arctic Clothing Company's bookkeeping system was simple, but effective.

Number 124 *Consider setting up a one-write system for handling checks.* With this system, which uses carbon paper and win-dow envelopes, the checks you write are automatically posted to a ledger. The system costs only a few hundred dollars to establish, and it soon pays for itself in the time it saves.

Number 125 *You should also organize a filing system during the first 60 days.* One way to have an effective filing system is to divide everything on a functional basis. For example, have a section for each of the following functional areas: marketing, production, finance, administration, and purchasing. Separate files will also be needed for bank documents and stockholders' correspondence.

Arctic carefully maintained separate files for correspond-ence from supply officers and army inspectors.

Number 126 *Any stationery store will have a basic accounting book that will assist you in keeping your records.* Buy one of these books and make sure that you keep track of receipts, sales, checks paid, people who owe you money (accounts receivable) and people you owe money to (accounts payable).

Several old metal files can probably be purchased from a used-furniture store for about $40 each. Filing cabinets should always be fireproof and well lined.

Arctic's records were stored in a metal box made by a local blacksmith.

Number 127 *Every new company and its managers need health and inventory insurance.* Even a service company will need limited inventory insurance. Without insurance, a severe fire or theft will bankrupt all but the best-financed new company. For as little as $300 a year, you can protect yourself from disasters of this type.

In 1811, the best insurance was a large family to protect the premises.

Number 128 *Find an insurance agent you trust to work with instead of constantly listening to proposals from a variety of agents.* Insurance agents can waste a great deal of your time. Pick one you like and send the others on their way.

Pierre La Rousse relied on his several sons and brothers to protect company property.

Number 129 *Use the Yellow Pages to find suppliers.* Instead of running all over town to talk to potential suppliers, save time by doing your preliminary screening by phone. Check the front of the Yellow Pages to cross reference products or suppliers.

In 1811, word of mouth substituted for the Yellow Pages.

Number 130 *An entrepreneur should be able to shift projects smoothly if a particular project runs into trouble or he loses interest in it.*

Pierre La Rousse, Arctic's president, had various alternatives in mind for outfitting the military.

Number 131 *At the end of each month, review for one hour what progress has been made during the month and assess the position of the company.* This will keep you from getting so bogged down in detail work that you lose sight of the forest for the trees. This kind of review is especially useful in assessing the financial resources of a company and the best way to organize it.

Each investor in the Arctic Clothing Company met with company officials once a month. Napoleon's chief supply officer met weekly with the company president.

Number 132 *Send a monthly report to your private investors with a copy to your bank loan officer.* Often a bank that makes you a loan will require that you send them a monthly report. In most cases private investors will not require regular reports, but will insist that the Board of Directors be informed about how things are going. Nevertheless, a monthly report to investors is a good idea. It lays the ground work for requests for additional funds and maintains their interest in the organization. Don't, however, spend so much time with investors that you don't have enough time to work on company business. By answering investors' questions, a monthly report can often save you time. It should at least reduce the number of phone calls you receive from nervous investors or from investors who feel they are not being kept up to date on the company's activities.

A good report might have the following sections:

1. Progress this month
2. Actual sales versus planned sales
3. Difficulties encountered
4. Corrective actions and suggestions
5. Plans for the following month

Both the French government and the Bank of Paris insisted

on a monthly progress report from the Arctic Clothing Company.

Number 133 *Avoid legal suits by settling disputes out of court.* A small company that is being sued (possibly for patent infringements or a failure to pay its bills) often finds it advantageous to try to settle the suit out of court rather than spend time and money on legal wrangling. Often, in a court battle, the new manager's ego is so involved in the suit that more funds are spent on legal costs than is justifiable from the standpoint of operations.

Many small companies have been bankrupted by excessive legal fees. Had they tried to settle, even though they did not save all they might have saved by going to court, they would have been better off. Being the plaintiff in a suit can cause problems too. Several companies such as Telex and Memorex sued IBM for patent infringements. However, such suits can go on for many years, and large firms like IBM can outlast small ones.

Several French firms threatened Arctic with suits claiming it copied their clothing designs. Pierre La Rousse sent his brother, the wrestling champion, to investigate the claims, which were subsequently withdrawn.

Number 134 *During the first few months of a new company, it is still very important to keep potential investors interested in it.* Several people who were unable to invest in the company initially may continue to show some interest in it. You should include these people on your mailing lists. Many venture-capital firms may fall into this interested observer category. Most venture-capital firms view themselves as second-round sources of financing. They will not help new companies, but will consider investing in them when the companies need funds.

Two people who did not invest in Arctic at the beginning did lend it money at a later date.

Number 135 *It's important to concentrate on marketing, as well as production and organization, from the very start.* Even if the company's products are not fully developed, you should establish some contact with potential buyers. Let them know you're around and what you hope to do.

Arctic's president and general manager wined and dined Napoleon's supply officers often in the initial months.

Number 136 *Remember that the long-term success or failure of a company cannot be predicted in 60 days.* Many entrepreneurs go rushing off expecting that in two months they will know whether their company will be successful and their products profitable. It is very, very rare for this to occur. In most cases, a minimum of three years is needed for a company's managers to know whether they have a long-term success on their hands. Several venture-capital firms will observe a company for years before making a judgment about its staying power.

Arctic knew that, since Napoleon could not keep attacking Russia indefinitely, its long-term success would depend on its finding private customers too.

five

Product development

"It is always growing weather."
Pierre Van Paasen

In view of recent droughts in California it is only appropriate to consider a company that removes salt from seawater as a possible new business.

Number 137 *Plan from the start to provide a balanced product line to your customers.* While it is important to concentrate on one or two products or services, try to provide a balanced product line. Give careful consideration to the needs of the accounts you are going to sell your product or service to in deciding what to offer. The organizers of the Pure Water Company should consider the needs of both industrial and residential users of water in marketing the firm's services.

Number 138 *Set a definite pattern and schedule for the development and introduction of each of your products.* It may be that you'll have to extend a product development and introduction phase for as long as three years. A schedule will help you keep on target. Pure Water is planning a three-year program to build a desalinating plant and pumping stations.

Number 139 *Obtain at least three quotes before making any purchases of materials not only in the product-development phase but after production begins.* Because prices and supplies vary widely, even for the same product, securing three price quotations before making any purchase is mandatory. A company can save money and survive by purchasing materials wisely. If necessary, hire a part-time workforce to assist you in obtaining price quotations. Free-lance professional people and students are a prime source of assistance for any small company. Placing an ad in a local student paper or putting a little 3 × 5 card on a university bulletin board will often attract enough student assistants at reasonable rates. Pure Water's part-time workers obtained excellent prices on the plastic piping needed to feed water into the desaltinating plant.

Number 140 *A new company must constantly think of who its market is and what they need in developing products.* For example, if your market is college students, it may be that while you're developing your main product you can offer posters or T-shirts to balance your product line. This approach will bring in additional funds that can be put to good use. Several of Pure Water's potential industrial users do not need water as pure as its residential customers require.

Number 141 *Keep a file of part-time employees.* As we mentioned above, part-time employees are a valuable resource. In searching for part-time assistants, you may run into individuals whose talents you do not need at the moment but who would be useful at a later stage. For this reason, it is very important to keep a file of potential part-time employees. One company we are familiar with uses a part-time commercial artist from an advertising agency. This individual prepares promotional drawings for $20 each and assists the company with its copy work and small ads.

All Pure Water's artwork will be done by moonlighting artists. They will be part of a program to inform the public of the desalinating program.

Number 142 *During the product development and introduction phase, limit all conversations with well-meaning friends.* This may seem like a simple recommendation, but often, while you're working on a new product or developing a product line, you will get calls from well-meaning friends with suggestions. It is helpful to listen to them, but only for a short time. Otherwise you may soon find yourself wasting half a day, a day or two or three days, being a sounding board for people who think they're being helpful.

Pure Water's president had his secretary interrupt him whenever "friendly" calls lasted more than a few minutes. Despite a feverish work pace, not all target dates were being met for the Pure Water Company.

Number 143 *Always obtain a signed release for photographs and artwork.* It is very important to get a signed release from a photograph's subject before the photograph is published. A simple form saying that the subject relinquishes all rights to the photograph and that he or she will file no claim in the future for royalty payments should be sufficient. The time to obtain such a release is when the photograph is taken.

Pure Water's photographer, Emily Calhoun, took numerous pictures of the plant and obtained signed releases from all the employees in the pictures.

Number 144 *If you use an overseas production company, have an independent company oversee the inspection and testing of the supplier's work.* If you work with overseas suppliers, it is very important to protect the quality of your products by requiring strict adherence to detailed specifications. There are companies in Japan and Taiwan that will inspect merchandise for you. They will work on contract for any U.S. company and often use very effective sampling procedures for ensuring product quality. For example, specify that if they sample 100 units of a product which are *unacceptable* based on your specifications, you can *reject* the whole lot. Many manufacturers in the Far East are quite familiar with this kind of arrangement. As long as you are running large quantities, the total end unit cost of having the goods inspected will be minimal. Generally, the inspection company will start working with the manufacturer before the products are made. This may sound a little bit like collusion, but the inspection company's reputation and future business depend on its doing a good job for you. Many overseas inspection companies work for the Department of Defense and have developed a good reputation over the years.

Some of Pure Water's plastic pipe will be imported from Taiwan. The International Inspection and Testing Company will make on-site tests of the pipe's quality in Taiwan.

Number 145 *In calculating rough costs for a product made overseas, add 20% to the cost of the product when it leaves the plant, wherever that is.* For example, if a product costs $1 leaving the plant in Japan, figure that your landed cost in the United States will be $1.20. This is obviously just a rule of thumb, but it is a useful way to calculate freight and duty rates rapidly. This add-on rule applies if the duty rate on the imported product is between 0 and 10%. For products on which the duty is higher than 10%, for example, cotton clothing, on which the duty is 20%, you should add an appropriate amount. In calculating the cost of cotton clothing, then you would add 30% to the cost of the product overseas, the normal 20% plus an additional 10% for the higher duty.

Pure Water estimated that its plastic pipe would cost $4 per foot leaving the plant and $.80 per foot (20%) more to cover miscellaneous charges.

Number 146 *If you're delegating product development and introduction work, make sure to review the work at least once every two days.* It is important to do this to motivate the people doing the work. You also need to keep informed about work you are having your own staff complete and be able to gauge when it will be ready.

Wesley Carem, Pure Water's president met daily with each of the foremen to assess their progress.

Number 147 *Plan for each new product's uniqueness.* The normal procedure in developing a new product is to make several changes in existing products. However, it is very important to consider just how unique your product or service will be. Merely making a slight improvement or change in an existing service or product will usually not be enough to get people to buy from you rather than their current suppliers. You have to make a substantial change so that your product or service appears truly unique.

Pure Water's process for removing salt from seawater was very unique.

Number 148 *Study an industry's basic pattern before developing a new product.* Review all the library materials available on your industry. It may be different in various ways you must consider before developing and introducing your product. For example in the ski business retail buyers make purchases in the spring for fall deliveries and pay for the merchandise the following January. This method of operation is called *seasonal dating,* and a ski industry supplier must be strong enough financially to work within its constraints.

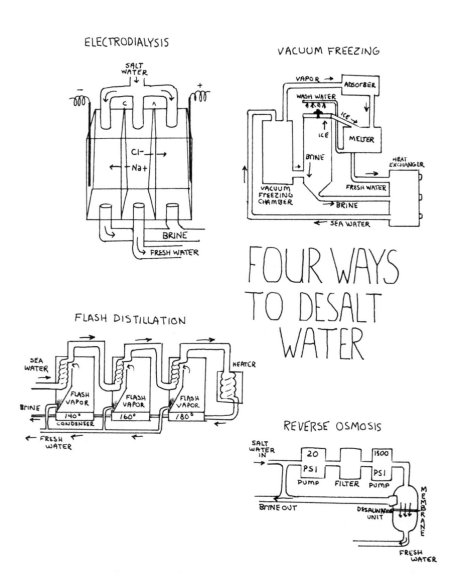

ELECTRODIALYSIS

VACUUM FREEZING

FLASH DISTILLATION

FOUR WAYS TO DESALT WATER

REVERSE OSMOSIS

Pure Water's president has studied reports of several previous attempts to devise economical desalinating methods.

Number 149 *Before developing a new product, try to visit an industry trade show to see existing products.* Most industries have an annual trade show. (New York and Chicago are favorite locales for this kind of thing.) Industry sales people, other company representatives, and accounts or stores that buy from them, all attend these shows. If you are fortunate enough to visit one before you get involved in a product's development or introduction, you will see whether there are any similar products or services available and also how they are sold. If you are unable to attend the show, try to learn about industry shortcuts and operating rules of thumb from discussions with other suppliers or manufacturer's representatives.

Several chemical plants were models for Pure Water's desalinating plant. Wesley Carem visited numerous chemical industry trade shows before approving his own plant's final design.

Number 150 *Have a detailed marketing plan for each of your products or services (if you only have a few).* If you have many products or services, write a detailed marketing plan for each product line. A step-by-step procedure for marketing a product will often give you ideas and help structure the product development phase.

Pure Water had a detailed plan for marketing desalinated water to local municipalities before work even began on its desalinating plant.

Number 151 *If you are developing a retail product, visit retail stores.* This can be a once-a-month activity. Often you can learn from the way products are packaged, priced and displayed in stores how to package and sell your own product.

Pure Water discussed selling bottled water through retail stores, but the competition and high shipping costs have discouraged it from going abroad with the idea.

Number 152 *Know whether your industry is a high-risk industry or one in which fads are prominent.* In industries such as the semiconductor industry, which is a high-risk industry, you can get stuck with high inventory of a particular item and be forced to take a substantial loss. In a high-risk industry it behooves you to be several steps ahead of what other companies are doing in the marketplace. In the clothing industry, which is faddish, it is very important to consider that most products will not last more than two seasons and make your plans accordingly.

A desalinating plant is a high-risk enterprise in that heavy rains and snow may sometimes eliminate the need for desalinated water.

Number 153 *Always keep a list of new products and the priorities you have assigned to them even if the priorities change.*

Pure Water has made a list of products that are spin-offs from its research into desalinating water. It hopes that several of these products can be sold to swimming pool owners.

Number 154 *In product development, a technical advisor who has experience in getting the job done is preferable to one who has only technical experience.*

A professor at UCLA who was an expert in chemical plant engineering and actually assisted in the construction of two plants was Pure Water's principal technical advisor.

Number 155 *Fear is a strong motivator for many new purchases.* In considering a product, decide whether it will allay customers' fears. For example, motorcycle theft insurance reduces the fears many individuals have that their bikes will be stolen.

The fear of not having enough water or of contaminated water would motivate many people to buy desalinated water.

Number 156 *Quantifying data is a necessity in developing new products.* Not only will this force you to throw out ideas for products that simply cannot be produced at a reasonable cost, it will also force you to estimate your costs as you go along.

The gallons of water used by each community in its area was the most important figure for Pure Water.

Number 157 *Legal restrictions on any product or process must also be considered.* It's important not to fall into the trap of developing an excellent product or service and then be blown out of the water by being sued the first time you try to sell it.

Most of the legal restrictions Pure Water encountered had to do with the location of its plant.

Number 158 *Never invest in any product or project the first three times you hear about it or discuss it.* Time is needed to adjust to and think over the information provided. Most projects are not so rushed that you need to make an immediate decision to invest in them.

The gestation period for the idea of desalinating water was five years.

Number 159 *If you have a choice between perfecting a product to the nth degree or marketing it, always go for marketing it.* Many entrepreneurs fall into the trap of refining their product to the point where it is so technical or expensive that it's difficult to produce. The development phase is so time consuming that the product never makes it to the market.

Pure Water began selling local communities on its product well before all the kinks in the desalination process were ironed out. As we have hinted in this chapter, developing a new product leads to higher highs and lower lows than many other human endeavors. There may be pain and frustration, but it may all be forgotten if you are successful. A friend of mine who set his kitchen on fire testing a product went on to sell 20,000 units of it.

six

New product decisions

"Anybody can cut prices, but it takes brain to produce a better article."

P. D. Armour

Dragons were a symbol of evil in the ancient world. In Greek mythology they were slain by Hercules, Apollo, and Perseus. Some dragons died young; some died old. However, there was a fate worse than death, life as an impotent dragon, unable to belch fire. In this chapter we will talk about Fire Starters, Inc., a company that seeks to manufacture fire starters for impotent dragons.

Number 160 *It is important for an entrepreneur to understand where new product ideas come from and how products arrive at the marketplace.* New products have a variety of sources. Among the six most likely sources are:

1. the marketplace
2. friends
3. customers
4. "fooling around"
5. new materials
6. technological changes

The idea of Fire Starters was first mentioned at the monthly meeting of the Friends of Dragons Society.

Number 161 *Even though you have a superior product or service, you may not be able to penetrate the market.* Why is that? Marketing has a lot to do with the success of a product. For example, an adhesive by the name of Pib was developed shortly after World War II, in 1948. It was far superior to anything else on the market. However, the effort made to sell Pib was very weak. There was no advertising or promotion, and the company that developed the product soon went out of business for lack of sales. You should not assume that because you have the best product available, sales will automatically occur. Many new ideas take a long time to catch on and your idea may be ahead of or behind its time.

Fire Starters would have to be marketed carefully, since impotent dragons are notoriously shy. A lack of blackened trees in their area is a sure giveaway that they have need for the product.

Number 162 *Most new products go through the following sequence or process before they are eventually refined enough so that they can be put on the market.*

1. Suggestion
2. Development
3. Testing
4. Refinement
5. Additional testing
6. Initial review of production
7. Detailed costing
8. Go-ahead decision

Fire Starters went through this process several times.

Number 163 *People who are thinking about starting a new* *company should always be alert for new products.* If they are not generating at least *one new product idea per week,* company presidents should consider the process by which ideas are coming to them. Their reading or their circle of friends may be simply too limited to provide many ideas.

Fire Starter's president had several ideas on the drawing board when he founded the company.

Number 164 *Visiting local stores to see what other products exist at comparable prices is an excellent way to test a new product idea.*

The idea of Fire Starters was approved by three retail store managers.

Number 165 *Making a mock-up of a product and taking it to the buyer of a local store can help you determine whether your idea has merit.*

Several Fire Starters were offered in local stores, but none were for dragons.

Number 166 *Don't be surprised if you have to make several changes in your product before it is marketable.*
Fire Starters were originally a liquid, and then a spray. The manufacturer finally concluded that the pellets were the best form in which to offer the product.

Number 167 *Normally if there is a market for a product and you have a good idea, all production problems can be solved.* Generalizing is dangerous; but it is usually true that if it is possible to generate a market for a product, it is possible to produce it.
Most of production's problems for Fire Starters were solved without too much difficulty.

Number 168 *During the production planning phase you should talk to at least four or five people who are knowledgeable about the production of your kind of product.* Most people fear that others will steal their ideas if they mention them. However, production people tend not to be too interested in marketing. Therefore, although there are some risks in showing your idea to them, they are usually minimal.
Several alchemists gave the Fire Starter project valuable assistance.

Number 169 *Always prepare a bill of materials or a full costing for your particular product or service.* Any library will have a book on production with sample bills of materials. Basically, all these are lists of the parts that go into a product and the production costs associated with each part. For example, to draw up a bill of materials for the digital taxi meter mentioned in an earlier chapter, you would simply list on the left-hand side of the page all the components needed to make the final product, including assembling of parts and the case. On the right-hand side of the page, you would list the cost and the number of units of each part in the final product.

Fire Starter pellets would cost $1.78 each and contain 16 chemical elements.

Number 170 *Do not, repeat, do not produce any units until you are sure customers will accept a product.* Test your product and keep your costs as low as possible.

This was a huge problem for Fire Starters. No consumer testing could be done since no dragons wanted to admit they needed the product.

Number 171 *Throughout the entire process of generating an idea, keep in mind that you must have a unique product or service to sell.* If you find halfway through the process that your product for the same cost merely duplicates others on the market, abandon it immediately. If you cannot come up with an alternate design or a way of improving the product to give it a significant advantage over similar goods, it isn't worth producing.

We're convinced that Fire Starters for impotent dragons was a unique product.

Number 172 *In considering a product for the retail market, always assume that a store will expect 50% of the retail price of products costing up to $20 and of products costing over $20, 40% of the retail price.* A sample costing for a child's silk-screened T-Shirt is shown below:

Shirt	-	$ .92
Screening	-	.25
Plastic bag	-	.03
Header card	-	.08
Manufacturer's cost		$ 1.28
Margin	-	.64
Wholesale cost		$ 1.92
Retail cost		$ 3.98

Each of Fire Starter pellet's cost $1.78 and would retail for $3.59. A package of five pellets would also be offered.

Patents

Number 173 *Consider that it may not be worth obtaining a patent for your product since the review process for a patent application takes up to three years.* If a product is a good idea it can usually be "designed around" by a competitor using slightly different components. Someone else may have to dominate the market while you are trying to protect your product through a patent. (See Appendix C for patents, inventions, and technology information on transfer.)

We expected that this formula for Fire Starters would be patented but that the process would take a long time.

Number 174 *If a product is fully developed and ready to go, it may be better to depend on marketing to give you the control you want over your market rather than a patent application.* If you talk with experts in the computer field, they'll admit that the rate of technology in their industry makes patents sometimes not worth applying for. In some industries, however, a patent may be valuable. It's important to consider the rate of change in your industry and the ease with which a competitor can "design around" your patent.

Number 175 *If you decide to file a patent using a patent attorney, plan on spending at least $700.* This would include the cost of drawings of the product and the write-up to be sent to the Commissioner of Patents.

Abe Collins, a patent attorney, gave an estimate of $1,100 for filing a patent application for Fire Starters.

Number 176 *To obtain a book on patents, contact any branch of the Government Printing Office or write directly to the Commissioner of Patents in Washington, D.C.*

The president of Fire Starters obtained a book from the Government Printing Office.

Number 177 *You can obtain sample patents and patent drawings from a patent library.* To find one, look in the white pages of the telephone book under "U.S. Government Patent Office."

Number 178 *If you wish to apply for your own patent, you should review at least 50 or 60 recent patents at a patent library.* This will let you see what you need to do to file the forms.

Files containing several sample patent application were reviewed by the president of Fire Starters.

Number 179 *Once you have filed for a patent, you can put "patent pending" on all your advertising, including header cards for your product.* Though it will not offer you any legal protection, this will make anyone else think twice about trying to patent a very similar product, since your patent will be first in line.

Once a patent application is filed, "patent pending" will be used on all Fire Starter materials.

Number 180 *If you see a product on the market that has "patent pending" on it and is very similar to your product, you should still consider going ahead with your product.* It pays to do so because if there is a similar products suit and you lost it, *the most that you could be required to do would be to pay a 3% or 4% royalty.* Usually your finances will be able to stand this if the market is strong enough to support your product and the competitor.

There were no competitive products when Fire Starters were introduced.

Trademarks

Number 181 *A trademark is often more valuable than a patent and can be obtained at a relatively low cost.* A trademark protects the name you use to sell your product. For example, if you call your product "Super Steel," you are able to protect the name "Super Steel" provided no one else has filed a prior application for that particular trademark. Applications for trademarks are usually acted upon much faster than applications for patents. It is possible to hear within a year or 18 months whether you are to be granted a particular trademark.

Number 182 *The cost of applying for a trademark is considerably less than the cost of filing for a patent. This is another reason you should consider setting a trademark first.* If you do all the work yourself (the forms are fairly simple), your total costs may be between $40 and $50. Trademarks are classified in certain ways, and for special classes the fee may be slightly higher.

The trademark "Scorch Plus" would cost about $150.

Number 183 *A trademark will generally increase the value of your company.*

It is estimated that the trademark "Scorch Plus" would double the value of the Fire Starter Company.

Number 184 *For information regarding trademarks you can write to the Commissioner of Patents in Washington, D.C., or look for a local federal office that has a federal bookstore associated with it. You can purchase a summary book on trademarks for about two dollars.*

The "Scorch Plus" company's president had the book on trademarks.

seven

Employees and personnel management

"A good listener is not only popular everywhere, but after awhile he knows something"

Wilson Mizer

Sooner or later, if a new company is going to grow, the founders must rely on work done by other people. Often this transition point is when problems begin. Usually, it's not the fault of either the founders or the new people involved that problems occur. A period of adjustment is normal as new employees learn to handle their jobs.

Most company founders know the value of job applications, job descriptions, and interviews in selecting and hiring new employees. However, the personnel job doesn't stop once a new individual is on board. It's still necessary to give consideration to:

- □ training (both on-the-job and formal) to upgrade employees' skills
- □ health and welfare plans (including the workmen's compensation plans required by most states)
- □ compensation and financial incentives (salaries, bonuses and commission rates).

Sensitive and fair personnel policies are important in securing loyalty and cooperation from your employees. No matter how much you have to do, you should find time to think about their needs.

In this chapter, we will use Driveway Blankets, Inc., a manufacturer of electric blankets to melt snow on residential driveways, as an example.

Number 185 *Keeping in mind that a new employee obviously cannot do a job as well as the company's founder will save you much aggravation and frustration.* No matter how capable new employees are, it usually takes them 30–60 days to learn their jobs. During this time it is important not to pressure them excessively or fire them for minor mistakes. However, if an employee will obviously never be able to do his or her job, he or she should be let go immediately.

Harry Colson, Driveway's president, has been slowly training several new employees.

Number 186 *In deciding what part you as the founder should play in a small company, consider the role of the benevolent dictator.*

One of the major problems in a large organization today is motivating its staff. A distinct advantage of small companies is that their staffs can observe all the operations of the company directly. Studies have shown that the staffs of small companies don't mind an authoritarian manager because they can see what role they are playing in the overall operation of the business and are aware of what's happening in and to the whole firm. In a large departmentalized company, the individuals in a particular area may be totally unaware of what's going on in the president's mind or the value of their own work to the company.

Driveway Blankets' president is in full control of the company's operation and keeps all his employees informed about it.

Number 187 *Be an enthusiastic manager, interested in what your employees are doing.* Make it a point to ask them one or two good questions, not try and pry into what they're doing, but to be of assistance as they go about their everyday tasks. A small company works best when the manager sets an example of concern. A calm questioning approach is very helpful in attempting to find out how employees are doing.

Harry Colson, Driveway's president, trys to spend some time each day helping new employees.

Number 188 *Motivating the accounting staff. Respect the training your bookkeeper or CPA has, but don't be a pushover in the financial area.* Nothing can destroy an investor or a bank's confidence in a small company faster than poorly kept books and poor judgment in financial matters. Always keep track of what your accountant or bookkeeper is doing.

Driveway's president meets with his accountant every Monday morning to review the firm's finances.

Number 189 *Spot-check various accounts.* For example, audit the major accounts for major receivables. Check the receivables over a certain dollar amount, and compare the amount on the books with the original invoices. This is probably a 20-minute job you should do once every two weeks.

Driveway's president reviews several accounts each Monday and often calls the account to verify the amount owed.

Number 190 *A company manager should also do internal auditing.* It is of primary importance to make sure that cash receipts on any particular day equal the amount entered in the books. It is also important that the firm's bank account be reconciled monthly. The manager of a new company should make sure this is being done regardless of whether its bookkeeping is handled by an outside bookkeeper or the firm's own staff.

Mr. Colson likes to check Driveway's cash receipts two days a week.

Number 191 *Many banks will set up programmed accounting programs for small companies that cost as little as $250 per month.*
Driveway Blankets, Inc., uses the First National Bank of Chicago's accounting program, which costs roughly $350 per month. Several special reports are prepared.

Number 192 *Motivating Marketing Staff. Avoid criticizing your representatives or salespeople.* The sales function in any company requires that the sales staff deal with the outside world. Buyers are often unreceptive to new ideas, and your representatives need as much support as possible. They may have to put up with frequent rejections during the day and turndowns. They will look to their own organization for support and you should give it to them.
Driveway Blankets, Inc. holds a weekly sales meeting to encourage its sales staff.

Number 193 *Become a good listener.* It is very important to listen to your salespeople or your distributors talk about their problems. Often they will solve the problems by themselves after you have listened to their comments.

Number 194 *Explain to your other employees what a marketing representative's typical day is like.* In order to assist your marketing representatives or your sales staff, your other employees should have a pretty good feel for what it is like to be in sales.
A typical rep's day begins with his calling five to ten accounts in an attempt to get appointments for that day or three or four days in the future. He will probably get three or four turndowns out of those five to ten calls. The one or two

accounts he does get to see during the day often result in no sale. The rep has talked to probably seven or eight people during the day, maybe even as many as 20 and may have nothing to show for his efforts. Therefore, it is important to support his morale, praising his efforts and raising intelligent questions as to what each account is doing. This will help you and your internal staff understand how each rep has handled his sales calls.

Carson McPeters, Driveway's general sales manager, gave a two-hour seminar on a marketing representative's day in September.

Number 195 *In working with your employees, you should first praise one or two things they are doing well.* It's doubtful that any individual is doing everything wrong. After praising the things they are doing well, you can then discuss areas where there is room for improvement.

In employee quarterly reviews, Driveway Blankets' president always compliments people on whatever they do well.

Number 196 *Motivating the Production Staff. Production standards are a very useful management tool in a small company.* These standards should be set carefully and changed infrequently. Working with your employees (not using a stopwatch) and initially doing the work yourself is a good way to come up with a reasonable production standard. Although the standard may be tighter than one the employees alone would set, the fact that they participated in setting it will help them feel that it is reachable. The fact that a manager was not "too good" to work on a project himself also boosts morale.

Some of these comments may give gray hairs to old-line psychologists and production people who have studied ways to get the maximum effort from employees. However, our experience has been that any new group of employees will more than likely include several who have outside interests

and will appreciate standards that let them know how much work is expected of them. From an employee's point of view, standards eliminate anxiety about how much work should be done in a day.

Another benefit of having production standards is that supervision costs are lower since employees seem to show much more initiative than they do without standards. Set-up costs are also lower because employees get themselves and the work area organized to start immediately. Finally, without production standards it is very difficult to estimate how much each product should cost or what customers should be charged.

Driveway expects its factory to turn out 200 electric blankets per day. Responsibility for each blanket's components is allocated among various work stations, and the employees understand what level of effort is expected of them.

Number 197 *Given the opportunity to work with production standards, employees may or may not wish to make extra money for exceeding a particular standard.* On some days certain employees are going to want to work faster than others. Occasionally, too, they will want to have a leisurely day and not work as hard. With reasonable production standards, it is possible not only to earn extra money for extra work but to have occasional lazy days, while still doing what is expected.

Some of our Driveway's employees work fast enough to go home two or three hours earlier than others.

Number 198 *Consider giving your employees the option of either earning extra money or going home for the day once a production standard is reached.* In one company we know of, employees bored with a very boring job would spend their time thinking of ways to harass the warehouse foreman. There was friction between the foreman and the employees and, although the work was getting done, the production standard was creating a heavily charged, troublesome atmosphere. The company solved the problem by offering people the opportunity to go home once a certain output had been achieved. This was contrary to normal procedures, which emphasize producing as many units each day as possible. However, in this case, morale in the plant improved drastically and, after a while, only a few people actually took the opportunity of going home early.

Driveway Blankets, Inc. gives its employees the option of leaving early or earning extra pay once its production standards have been reached.

Number 199 *It may be particularly useful for companies that have a very seasonal operation to set up this kind of arrangement.*

At Driveway once 200 electric blankets have been produced in a day, the production employees may go home.

Number 200 *Getting people to work for you and getting them to work hard for you is easier if you hire the right people to begin with.* Industrial psychology offers two basic theories as to when individuals will perform well. One is that people will work well if they understand what they are doing and why their job is important. The other theory is that employees will work well if they are told to do their jobs or else (if they fear being fired for shirking). Another approach is based on the employees' self-interest. Its basic tenet is that to get people to work hard for you, you first have to find out what their interests and needs are. Unless a job satisfies their interests and needs, neither fear nor persuasion will prevent them from eventually moving on to something else.

Many of Driveway's employees are students who work during the peak production time in the summer. The job meets their needs since it's part-time, short-term work.

Number 201 *To match people and jobs successfully you must find out whether they really want part-time or full-time work, whether they like working with numbers or people, and whether they want a position in which hard work may lead to advancement, or one they can forget about at five o'clock.* If you find these things out during your interviews with job applicants, you will be able to hire the most suitable people from among those with the qualifications you require.

Driveway Blankets has no morale problems since most of the less skilled jobs are done by summer employees who are glad to have temporary work.

Number 202 *Never lie about a job.* In a company with which we are familiar, one of the managers had a job to fill that was strictly typing, with a small amount of filing for seven hours a day. The manager thought about various ways to vary the content of the job and eventually added some telephone selling. However, the job was still mostly typing. Several individuals were hired for the position, but they did not work out because they were unhappy doing typing.

In interviewing further applicants the manager decided to describe the job as a full-time typing job. Eventually, a very helpful, loyal employee was found who liked to type. The moral of this story is that by considering an individual's likes and dislikes before hiring him or her, you can make everybody happy.

As we have pointed out, Driveway's production employees don't mind doing very monotonous jobs, such as typing or assembly-line work, since they are mostly summer employees who will be doing something else in a few months.

Number 203 *Newspapers are generally not that effective a source for new employees.* Contrary to what most people think, the best employees are seldom found through newspaper ads. Partly this is because such ads appeal to people who lack the initiative to find a job in other ways. It is fairly easy to buy a newspaper, open it and start making phone calls. However, it does work for some companies and may be effective for you.

Driveway Blankets does not use newspaper ads in seeking new employees.

Number 204 *The best sources of new employees are friends, acquaintances and present employees.* People recommended by your friends or employees are, in a sense, prescreened. Beware, however, of hiring someone you are not certain is suitable for a job simply because he or she is a friend. If you run into problems and have to fire the person, the ramifications can affect your personal life also.

Driveway Blankets has very few employees who are related. However, there are many friends of employees working for the company.

Number 205 *A second source for good employees is your support staff.* Almost every business has an accountant, a lawyer, and an insurance agent. These three individuals can often recommend people they have come in contact with for a position. The final decision though must be yours.

Driveway's support staff has recommended several very good employees.

Number 206 *A third good source of employees is the placement office at a local business school.* Individuals who have gone through local business schools are usually well motivated, in addition to having some training. The schools are very appreciative when an employer inquires about their graduates and will generally try to find someone suitable.

Hal Conway, the local business school placement officer, has referred several excellent employees to Driveway Blankets.

Number 207 *A fourth way of finding good people is to have contacts in the personnel departments of large companies.* Such contacts may be glad to refer to you people who wish to work only part time, or who do not wish to work for a large company. Some people find jobs in large companies too specialized. In a small company, a variety of duties may be handled by one person, such as an office manager, or a secretary-receptionist.

A nearby company, Harris, Inc., has referred several office personnel to Driveway Blankets.

Number 208 *Keeping Good People. It is best to give small, more frequent raises than to give one large raise at the end of the year.* In a small company, it's often touch and go as to whether the firm will survive. Raising employees' salaries every three or six months if the company is doing well is *more* effective in encouraging people to stay than having an annual salary review system.

When Driveway Blankets was started, each employee (there were very few) was reviewed every two months.

Number 209 *When promotions or changes in job functions occur, if possible, announce the changes in trade journals.* This is a very effective way to reward an employee since it gives the employee an opportunity to become better known in an industry. It also gives the company name more exposure.

When Cindy McDonald was promoted from a secretarial position at Driveway Blankets to office manager, the promotion was announced in the *Electrical Contractor News.* Cindy was exuberant!

Number 210   *Whenever possible, structure a job so that the holder has a title.* This is especially important in dealing with individuals who have been to college. For them, being hired to do filing is not very satisfying. It may be a little misleading to call people office operations managers rather than file clerks, but it may make them more interested in their work and more inclined to show incentive.

At the risk of sounding trite, it is very important to build a loyal team that works together. In a small company, the manager is very visible. Giving an employee a title and making him or her feel like part of the management increases one person's effectiveness. It often has other benefits as well. If, for example, an important customer comes in when the manager is out, the employee can present his or her card and offer to help.

Each of Driveway Blankets' office workers has the title of administrative assistant instead of secretary. And workers are, in fact, becoming true administrative assistants.

Number 211   *Listening carefully to what employees have to say at the beginning of each day is very valuable.* Often talking about a problem, verbalizing it, makes a person feel better and more able to deal with a day's work, even if no immediate solution to the problem emerges.

Harry Colson, Driveway's president, is very careful to talk with most of the company's regular employees at the beginning of each day.

Number 212 *It is very important to have a normal amount of humor in an office.* A very somber businesslike office simply doesn't appeal to most people. Getting things done is important and most employees work better in a pleasant atmosphere. Of course, good judgment is required, and there are limits to how relaxed one should be. Humor at someone else's expense is to be avoided.

Margaret Craven, Driveway Blanket's office wit, keeps everyone amused with her subtle humor while still doing her job and managing to lend a hand to new people.

eight

Importing and exporting

"Every fact that is learned becomes a key to other facts."

E. L. Youmans

Cleopatra was fond of floating down the Nile on a barge. Often strong waves would swamp the barge and ruin her outing. In this chapter we shall discuss a company that proposed to redesign Cleopatra's barge for smoother sailing, using new imported oars from Italy.

Number 213 *Any new company should study what importing and exporting is done in its particular industry with a view to increasing its profits.* Thanks to the efficiency of worldwide transportation and communication networks, importing and exporting offer a wide range of opportunities for new companies. You should at least review the import-export possibilities in your industry. Obviously, they will be more numerous if your company deals in products rather than services.

In Cleopatra's day there were many opportunities for imported products in the boat-building industry.

Number 214 *Advantages of Importing. A major advantage of importing products for U.S. firms is lower labor costs in many* *countries.* The Far East has long been noted for low labor costs. A current center of low-cost production is Taiwan, where many clothing items for major stores are now being made. For a long time, the semiconductor industry produced a large number of parts in Taiwan. Hong Kong also has many contracts from U.S. companies. J. C. Penney, for example, makes most of its clothing in Hong Kong. In the future, low-cost production may be centered in India and Singapore, where labor rates are as low as 10¢–15¢ a day.

For Cleopatra's new boat, we planned to use specially hewn oars from Italy. Italian labor costs at the time were substantially lower than Egypt's for that particular product.

Number 215 *A second major advantage of importing is that you can often find unique products in foreign countries.* This is especially true in Europe, where many high-quality products are made. European skis and bicycles, for example, are well known for their excellence.

In this case, the oars to be imported from Italy were unique.

Number 216 *Importing often offers a U.S. company the advantage of being the representative of an overseas company.* A U.S. company can be the sales branch for a multitude of products in the U.S. market. This particular advantage of importing should not be overlooked. Overseas companies have no interest in sending to the United States twice yearly a sales person who does not know the market as well as people who live in the United States.

Egyptian Boats, Inc. planned to be the exclusive representative of Italian Oars Limited.

Number 217 *Disadvantages of Importing. The founder of a new company should be aware that there are several disadvantages of importing, the major one being that, given a choice of similar products and prices, a buyer in the United States will always* _prefer a product made in the United States._ This comment applies not only to the consumer and user of a product but also to the department store buyer who decides which products the consumer will choose from.

Cleopatra, when reviewing the project, stressed that she would prefer Egyptian oars. However, she agreed to Italian oars when the smoothness of the ride they provided and the need to improve trade relations with the rest of the Roman Empire were discussed.

Number 218 _A second major disadvantage of importing is that although some products can be made more cheaply overseas, there may be high rates of duty on them which the U.S. importer must pay._ Often the differences in labor costs overseas are so significant that no amount of duty will be difficult for the importer to pay and still make money. However, duties occasionally are high. For example, the duty on clothing is 20% whereas the duty on locks is only 4.5%. On some electronic parts, the duty can be as high as 40%. Thus despite lower costs overseas, by the time you pay the duty and the freight to the United States you may have a noncompetitive product.

Working with the Egyptian queen directly had advantages. Cleopatra agreed to waive all duty on the Italian oars. Normally Egyptian Boats would have had to pay a duty of 25%.

Number 219 _Always, when importing from overseas, pay particular attention to the quality of the merchandise._ Once merchandise is shipped from overseas, it is very difficult to send it back if there is a problem. If you produce goods in the United States, it is fairly easy to send them back to the factory to have a problem corrected. If something is brought in from Japan or Taiwan, the cost of shipping it back for repairs may be prohibitive. The shipping cost often is a major portion of the product cost. On the other hand, some electronic companies that bring parts in from Taiwan are not bothered by a 5% to 10% rejection rate. It is still worthwhile to import the parts because of lower production costs overseas.

Occasionally, Roman woodsmen were known to use dull axes that splintered some oars. Normally, however, the quality of their oars was excellent.

Number 220 *Before you attempt importing, learn something about importing systems and procedures.* Familiarize yourself with the various reports, letters of credit, and duty requirements involved in processing merchandise entering the United States. After you have handled several transactions, the work will become fairly routine, since it follows a pattern. However, it does take a while to learn the mechanics of importing special products. Obtaining the right duty rate often has a large bearing on whether you can import a product profitably.

Egyptian Boats, Inc. hire an import specialist to handle overseas purchases.

Number 221 *The most effective way to find products for import is to list your company's name with trade associations in the country you wish to import from.* For example, if you wish to import from Taiwan, you should list your name with the trade associations there. About four or five weeks after the listing appears you should receive about 30 or 40 letters asking you to represent various companies in the United States. Often these letters are fairly general, saying that the trading company in Taiwan will provide any product you need. You can then, through correspondence divide the areas you wish to concentrate on. The Roman Trade Association gladly put Egyptian Boats, Inc., on its mailing list.

Number 222 *Another excellent way to find products is to talk to the commercial officer of the consulate of the country you wish to* *import from.* He or she will have books, statistical data, product samples, and pictures of certain products and industries. For example, the Italian commercial officer in most cities has a book of all Italian manufacturers and their products. After reviewing the book, you could write a series of letters to companies you were interested in and possibly begin import/ export activities with them. For a new company, it is often too expensive to fly to particular countries to find merchandise you would like to bring to the United States. Also, it takes time to find what you really want, time that might be better spent developing business in the United States.

One of Cleopatra's ministers discussed the importation of oars with the Roman Empire's commercial officer in Cairo.

Number 223 *The most effective way for many companies to start importing is to send a cable to the company with which they wish to do business.* Overseas companies seem to respond better to cables than to letters. Cables also arrive faster than letters.

Runners were used with messages from Egyptian Boats to Italian suppliers.

Number 224 *You can call RCA or Western Union, send an international cable to Japan or Taiwan, and receive an answer within 48 hours for $3.00.* In the long run a cable may even save you money since time is money when you are producing products and trying to develop markets.

Egyptian Boat runners took about one week (including time spent on ship board) to deliver messages.

Number 225 *When importing, try to find unique products that every other importer will not see or will not try to import.* If everybody is importing the same product or has seen it, your chances of doing well are very limited. Making slight changes in products or finding unique products will give you a better chance of surviving in the import business.

No other Egyptian importer was bringing in Italian-made oars.

Number 226 *An excellent way to find unique products is to attend trade shows and the traveling commercial shows that several countries sponsor.* For example, the Taiwan Chamber of Commerce sponsors a trade show in Los Angeles, Dallas, Chicago, and New York. If you are not near one of these cities, you can still call the hotel where the trade show will be and talk with an individual who represents the type of company or product you are looking for. Trade shows are an effective way of seeing what's new and also for generating contacts. They are an easy way to meet foreign business people who can be very useful to you when they go back home.

Egyptian Boats discovered its special Italian oars at a trade show in Cairo.

Number 227 *Methods of Payments—Using Letters of Credit. Find a good commercial bank with a strong international department for writing letters of credit to obtain overseas merchandise.* Most overseas business is done through letters of credit. Funds are set aside to pay for the overseas merchandise before it is made, but they are not transferred until the merchandise is delivered. The procedure is complete when a letter of credit is written and sent to an overseas bank, the supplier gets its money, and the buyer gets its merchandise.

The Bank of Cairo had a very strong international department and was able to assist Egyptian Boats with a letter of credit for the Italian oar maker.

Number 228 *In writing a letter of credit, one of the most important decisions is the currency to be used.* Make sure that you consider the long-term money market in writing the currency on letters of credit. Many companies write letters of credit in terms of U.S. dollars only. This allows them to state a fixed price and avoid problems caused by currency fluctuations. If you write a letter of credit in terms of the currency of the other country, you will feel the effects of currency fluctuations when converting back to dollars.

By guessing whether the dollar will get stronger or weaker in the three months or so before your letter of credit will be drawn on, you can speculate with respect to currency. If the dollar gets stronger, you will save on the product's price, as some importers of British goods did when the pound was dropping rapidly.

Egyptian Boats expected to write all letters of credit in Roman currency, which they considered weaker than Egyptian.

Number 229 *It is important to remember that the safest and probably the best way for a novice importer to write letters of credit is in U.S. dollars.* This way you won't have any problems with currency fluctuations. You'll know exactly how much the merchandise is going to cost you. After a while if you feel more adventuresome, you may wish to consider writing a letter of credit in the currency of the country you are buying the merchandise from.

Since Egyptian Boats is an Egyptian company, writing the letters of credit in Egyptian money was equivalent to writing them in dollars.

Number 230 *How to Physically Receive Merchandise. You can expect freight shipped from Europe and the Far East by ocean to take at least 15 to 18 days in transit.* You will have to add a week to either of those figures if you are going to the West Coast from Europe or from the Far East to the East Coast. Occasionally problems such as dock strikes, lost documents and ocean storms slow shipments down considerably. It is generally best to allow 30 to 45 days for merchandise to be delivered.

The shipping from Italy to Egypt was several days time during Cleopatra's reign.

Number 231 *The easiest way to receive merchandise in the United States is to pay for a freight forwarder's services.* In many port cities, such as San Francisco, New York, Boston and Houston, there are companies whose sole job is to handle merchandise and clear it through customs. They make sure all the paperwork is done, that the merchandise gets through customs, and that the duty is calculated properly, and have the merchandise trucked to you.

Egyptian Fast Freight, a local freight forwarder, was asked to handle Egyptian Boat's incoming merchandise.

Number 232 *Consider clearing small shipments through customs yourself instead of paying a freight forwarder to do it.* This may be especially feasible when merchandise is shipped by air since you can fill out the forms and do the paperwork necessary to clear the merchandise through customs at the airport. However, it is still advisable to use a freight forwarder for large shipments.

Egyptian Boats planned to clear small shipments of oars itself.

Number 233 *Estimating Costs. For merchandise received from overseas, use the 20% rule in estimating costs.* Given all the problem mechanics of importing, you may wonder how you begin to estimate for a particular customer and what the cost of merchandise is going to be. Usually if the duty rate is less than 12% it is best to use the 20% rule. In other words, in pricing a product for your customer, calculate that the merchandise is going to cost you 20% more than the price you are being quoted for the merchandise to be delivered to the dock in the country of manufacture.

In other words, if ski goggles delivered to the dock in

Hong Kong cost $2 and the duty is less than 12%, then your total landed cost for the merchandise in your United States warehouse should be approximately $2.40 per unit, or 20% above the cost. This may sound like a simple rule, but it is an important one to remember when you are talking with customers and have to come up with quick estimates on products.

Egyptian Boat's first shipment was to cost $3 million delivered to the dock in Italy. The anticipated total cost for the shipment was $3,600,000 (20%more).

Number 234 *If you are exporting, contact foreign governments' trade offices, which are usually located in the largest city of the country you are interested in, and obtain from them the names of trading companies with whom you can correspond.* Since the 1972 devaluation of the dollar, the export business has been a very attractive business for U.S. companies to explore. There are several ways in which a new company can become an exporter. In most countries, there are trading companies or export companies interested in trading with U.S. companies. In writing letters to them, always explain carefully how they will be able to make money from the transaction you propose.

Once Cleopatra's boat was finished, Egyptian Boats expected the export market and various trading companies to be valuable resources.

Number 235 *The Mechanics of Exporting. In your first efforts at exporting, always work with regular freight forwarders or companies that specialize in export/import arrangements.* Usually these companies are familiar with customs regulations and will prepare export and import documentation. The personnel of these companies can develop all the documentation for you, including the very important export declaration ("ex dec"). Often the freight forwarder you use for importing is also skilled in exporting and will be able to assist you.

Exporters of Cairo, an export specialist, worked with Egyptian Boats.

Number 236 *After you have had some experience with freight forwarders, you should explore the possiblity of preparing your own export declarations.* If you can eventually do your own paperwork, you will save money.

Egyptian Boats expected eventually to prepare its own export declarations.

Number 237 *In considering markets for your products, do not neglect small countries.* There is a tendency to figure that if you are going to export you should probably do so to Europe and Japan. Any information or trade requests you receive from the Phillippines or Malaysia should be disregarded. However, many companies have found that the *smaller* countries have an expanding number of potential buyers. Often, there are enough buyers for an aggressive trading company to develop a good business for you. In a smaller country too, a trading company usually has to work harder for its business and may therefore be more receptive to handling a new company, such as yours and your products.

Several newly formed countries with many rivers seemed to be ideal sales prospects for Egyptian Boats.

Number 238 *Exporting to Canada. In considering exporting, always consider Canada as a possible customer.* Often when people think about the world economy and the countries that it might be worthwhile to export to, they forget all about one of the easiest countries to reach and to deal with: Canada. Although its population is much smaller than that of the United States, it is still a good market for many U.S. products.

In Cleopatra's time, Canada was an unknown country.

Number 239 *Any large stationery store will have a supply of Canadian customs forms. It is a simple matter to fill out these forms with a little help from the U.S. customs office, which can tell you of the district and port through which the merchandise will be shipped.* The forms necessary for shipping merchandise into Canada are a standard export declaration and a Canadian customs invoice. The key items on each of these forms are the names of the shippers and the consignees. It's important to remember to *sign* the forms. Some companies have had interesting experiences spending considerable time with the customs people, organizing and preparing export forms, and then sending them out without the required signatures. Completing the Canadian form is basically a mechanical transaction, and if there are any other mistakes they can normally be corrected at the other end.

Another advantage in dealing with Canada is that the customs and needs of the people are very similar to those of U.S. citizens. If your product or service is popular in this country, it will more than likely be popular in Canada.

Egyptian Boats expected that a local stationery store would have customs parchment for neighboring countries.

Number 240 *Sometimes a government agency in a foreign country will be interested in upgrading the standard of living there by importing your products, even though the income of the average person makes it impossible to purchase your products.* Televisions have been sold in many developing countries as education tools for school systems, although people can't afford sets in their homes.

Cleopatra's Boat was actually to be sold to the Egyptian Government. Possibly in future years it would be made available for public uses.

Number 241 *Avoiding Pitfalls in Exporting. The greatest pitfall for a small company in exporting is to spend too much time trying to develop its international business.* You're in trouble if your secretarial staff is spending all its time doing research on potential overseas customers, sending cables overseas, and so on, while your U.S. business, which pays your overhead is being neglected.

Since Cleopatra expected her new boat to be delivered on time, Egyptian Boats spent very little time exploring export opportunities.

Number 242 *Before making any exporting decision, consider the timing of your decision.* This obviously applies to all aspects of business, but it is of critical importance in international business. For example, one particular ski-products company failed to understand that the Canadian ski business is different from the U.S. ski business. Canadian ski sales are not as closely geared to annual ski shows as is U.S. business. In the United States ski orders are placed in May or June and shipments are made in September. Canadian businesses are in no mood for purchasing ski merchandise until August or September, at which time they want immediate shipments. It is surprising how often matters of timing cause large mixups among firms trying to do business internationally.

Cleopatra liked to sail down the Nile in the spring and fall when the weather was cooler and was uninterested in buying boats in the summer or winter.

Number 243 *Before exporting any product, spend some time talking with local customs officials.* They will be able to assist you and may actually indicate several profitable export markets for your products.

Local customs officials may also suggest lower duty categories for your products.

Number 244 *Another "must" would be an interview for exporters with the individual in charge of exporting at the local Small Business Administration office.* One of the functions of the SBA is to assist U.S. companies interested in exporting their products. Also, being placed on the SBA's export list will entitle you to receive the names of foreign companies who express an interest in particular products through U.S. agencies in their country. Computer printouts of export requests are sent to all potential suppliers on the SBA's list. Following these leads can be helpful. Since many companies receive them, you should carefully assess your chances of success before making a competitive bid.

Cleopatra's government had a small export office that handled requests for Egyptian products and prepared export leads.

nine

Marketing and selling

"Be slow of tongue and quick of eye."
Cervantes

Marketing permeates *everything* a new company does. Even during detailed financial negotiations both the company founder and potential investors are constantly exploring marketing topics. The company we shall use as an illustration in talking about marketing should appeal to anyone who has ever studied the piano. The firm Music, Inc., manufactures computerized Bach players. To operate the players, you simply put them beside your piano and feed in some Bach sheet music. The tune is then played while the student listens. After the music stops, the student plays the piece on the piano.

Number 245 *Marketing involves more than just sales. It includes market research, product planning, pricing, advertising, merchandising, and packaging.* If you concentrate on sales alone, you may find yourself outflanked by someone with a new product or a lower price. You must pay attention to all aspects of marketing if you want your company to thrive. Your *market research* should include listening to comments from salespeople, customers, suppliers, and company employees. You should also read industry publications. At the end of each month it may be helpful to ask yourself, "What market research information have I received this month?" A formal *product review* and *product planning* schedule works best even in small companies. For example, you might decide to set aside two hours on the last Friday of each month for a product planning session. At this meeting you should proceed product by product, discussing strengths, weaknesses, marketplace acceptance, and actual sales. After the existing product line has been reviewed, new products can be proposed and considered. Chapters 5 and 6 list several points that should be discussed.

Pricing decisions are determined by marketplace conditions:

- ☐ What are competitors charging?
- ☐ How much is a product or service worth to customers?
- ☐ How much are customers able to pay?
- ☐ What does it cost the firm to produce the product?

You will notice that we mentioned costs last. One of the most frequent mistakes new companies make is to base the price of products *strictly* on their costs. *Always* start with marketplace conditions, not costs.

Advertising is covered in other parts of this book. For most small companies, press releases are the best and least expensive form of advertising. If you do advertise by other methods, try to avoid these common mistakes:

1. A poor choice of medium. (Trade magazines, not TV, are best for technical products.)
2. A one-shot approach. (Advertising works best if used consistently over a long period.)
3. A confused message (called *weak copy* in advertising jargon). Try to establish one or two product benefits

in the mind of the reader or listener. Don't tell him
every benefit!
4. Spending too much on advertising in relation to your
overall marketing plan. (Point-of-sale displays may
deserve equal dollars.)

While *merchandising* means many different things, most of
our comments will be related to shelf kits and in-store displays. Frequent visits to stores to review displays can be very
helpful. The combination of a good commercial artist and a
container company sales rep will teach the founder of a new
company more about *packaging* than many hours of independent study. You should plan to spend at least an hour each
week with such people.

Music, Inc.'s president, Murray Bonner, used to think of
himself only as a salesman. He is now learning to think of
marketing as more than just sales.

Number 246 *The heart and brains of a small business are the two
vital organs of a product program.* When the heart and brains
are functioning, the organism is healthy. Though a sound
heart and brain won't assure a long life, they are certainly
essential to it. The *heart* of a small business is what you take
to market (your products). The *brains* of a small business are
the prices you sell them for. The control of the heart and brain
in an entrepreneurial venture should never be left to someone
other than the founder or delegated to outside subcontractors.
For the venture to be viable, the entrepreneur must remain in
charge of the heart and the brains.

Music, Inc.'s management is in complete control of the
product line and pricing decisions.

Number 247 *Accept the fact that no matter what profession or
business you are in, you have to sell your products or services.*
That is not true, you may say; doctors and lawyers don't have
to sell their services. However, they do have to explain them.

Moreover, if they suggest an operation or a lawsuit, they must convince you that they can do the job.

Much of a doctor's or a lawyer's business comes from referrals, and much of their time is spent talking to patients or clients. By what they say to people, they are selling themselves.

Likewise, one who is applying for a job or explaining what he or she has done on a project to the boss is selling his or her ability and efforts.

Music, Inc. plans to sell its Bach players through various distributors and manufacturer's representatives.

Selling: Fun or Merely Effort?

Number 248 *Everyone in sales needs to develop a selling technique. What works for some people is to think of selling as requiring empathy with the customer, a system, and discipline.* To make a sale, a salesperson has to have a certain amount of empathy, enough to understand the customer's needs. The customer has to feel that he is getting what he or she needs from the salesperson and the salesperson's company. Rapport with a salesperson helps a customer feel comfortable about a sale.

Preferably, all Music, Inc.'s distributors will be people who have played the piano or have been very close to someone who has learned to play.

Number 249 *If you are selling a product it may be difficult to gain acceptance for, it is helpful to sell a few smaller companies first and then work on the larger accounts.* This is a sales system which can vary from industry to industry. Analyzing the marketplace in an industry usually leads to a profitable and useful system.

The smaller music stores will be the first target for Music, Inc.'s sales reps.

Number 250 *Develop a system that works by concentrating on particular types of accounts.* If you are selling tax-shelter investments, it may be helpful to concentrate on larger companies such as Fairchild, Ampex, Motorola, or General Electric.

Clearly music stores must be Music, Inc.'s first target, before general merchandise stores.

Number 251 *Most sales result from hard work.* It is almost trite to say this, but it is almost impossible to make a sale without making an effort to get the sale. Although some people are very lucky on occasion, most of their luck results from very hard work. Your salespeople should set definite hours to be out of the office and on the road calling on accounts. For example, several companies have found it helpful to specify that they would like to see their salespeople on the road no later than 8:30 in the morning. Some companies have even rewarded a salesman's wife for verifying that her husband was out of the house by 8:30 in the morning. This may be a rather extreme approach, but salespeople must discipline themselves to make a certain number of calls and not give up after five or six no's in a row.

Most of Music, Inc.'s distributors regularly call on six or seven music stores a day.

Number 252 *Most salespeople gain business because they are friendly, try to be helpful, and call on a particular account regularly.* This is especially true with regard to salespeople for trucking companies. Basically, they are all selling the same service. The person who works with and spends time with clients is usually the one who ends up receiving the business. Everyone has days when they don't feel like working, when they would rather be out having fun. Understanding this will make it easier for you to motivate yourself on those days when it seems like nothing is going to help you make a sale.

All Music, Inc.'s distributors are friendly with the music store people they call on regularly.

Almost Anyone Can Sell

Number 253   *To make a sale or to make a sales program work, you have to be convinced that you are going to make the sale or that the program will eventually work.* Obviously, there is a possibility that the sale won't occur or that the program won't work, but you can't proceed on this assumption. If you assume you will fail, you *will* fail.

Because of extensive market testing, the management of Music, Inc. is confident that the company's sales program will be successful.

Number 254   *It is a myth to think that because you are not an extrovert you cannot be a good salesperson.* Most salespeople are not and need not be extroverted. Their job is to provide service and assist their customers. Reminding yourself of this fact will make you feel more comfortable about the sales function.

The best potential Music, Inc. distributor concentrates on service and is not a very outgoing person.

Number 255   *Don't use the excuse that you can't live with rejections to avoid selling.* Most business people you talk with are friendly. They know that talking to salespeople gives them a chance to find out about new products that may be useful to their company. Most rejections are friendly and softened by such remarks as, "Well, let's try again with something different." A customer may even suggest how a particular salesperson might sell his or her company. There are very few out-and-out hostile rejections.

All Music, Inc.'s distributors have excellent records in selling other products.

Number 256 *Don't avoid sales or calling on accounts because you have convinced yourself that you can't pick up a phone and make a phone call.* This attitude occurs either out of fear that the phone call will produce a rejection or harsh words. Occasionally, you get into a pattern of worrying too much about how people will react to a call. It's important to turn your mind off if something needs to be done. Don't fall into the trap of thinking that other salespeople feel comfortable every single time they pick up the phone. Selling can be a very rewarding career if you approach it positively. In a lot of companies the salespeople are so important that they make considerably more than managers.

The two best salespeople at one of Music, Inc.'s distributors make $10,000 more a year than the national sales manager.

Number 257 *Keep in mind that the hardest part of any sales program is the first few calls.* Once you make a few calls and have a few good reactions, selling can be very exciting.

Music, Inc. expects a slow, initial acceptance of its product because of the importance of demonstrations to sales. Once shown the Bach players, however, people tend to be very enthusiastic about them.

Number 258 *Consider telephone selling as a means of covering more accounts for less money and in less time.* Many companies have found that listening to their accounts' problems on the phone is a faster and more economical way to do business. If they had to go out and see the accounts every time a problem came up, servicing them could be very expensive and time-consuming. The telephone should not always be a substitute for personal calls on accounts, but it often proves to be a more cost-effective way of servicing them.

Music, Inc.'s distributors will qualify prospects through telephone selling.

Selling Procedures

Number 259 *Analyzing the market for particular products, the accounts in the market (both large and small), and the estimated revenue from them is critical.*

Music, Inc. has made detailed studies of the music market, both stores and individual students, to develop revenue estimates.

Number 260 *A sales plan is a very important part of your overall marketing program.*

To save on overhead, Music, Inc. will sell its players through distributors and manufacturers' representatives.

Number 261 *Don't restrict yourself to selling large accounts because it may take too long to sell them.* It's important to have a mixture of large and small accounts in any particular area.

The larger music schools are targets for Music, Inc.'s products, but most of its business will come from small music stores.

Number 262 *It is important to set up a file for each potential account.* After reviewing the market and finding out who may be able to use your product, make up a simple card file for jotting down comments about each account. Instead of trying to remember what happened the last time you called on a customer, you can simply refer to your notes.

Each Music, Inc. distributor has a file on all the accounts in its territory.

Number 263 *Analyze carefully what your competitors are offering your customers.* Be prepared for comments from customers about what competitors are doing with their products. If you can show familiarity with a competitor's products and can demonstrate how your products are different and better, you may be able to overcome a customer's objections to trying them.

No one in the music industry is offering a product similar to Music, Inc.'s Bach players.

Number 264 *After making your sales calls, you should consider a monthly evaluation of your marketing plan.* Calling on accounts tells you about what's happening in a market. It's remarkable how much information you can obtain from even three or four sales calls. Use this information to regularly reevaluate your marketing strategies.

Music, Inc.'s management and distributors will make joint calls on music stores to help the firm regularly evaluate its sales strategy.

Selling: Myths vs. Reality

Number 265 *Salespeople are made, not born, and selling can be an exciting occupation.* It is true that not everyone can be in sales because some people don't have the *will* to become a salesperson or an *interest* in selling. It is also true that most people in sales *develop* their skills. They have been trained to sell and are not natural-born salespersons. Often, they choose selling as a job because it can be an extremely exciting occupation and allows you considerable freedom. For example, you can set your own schedule. Occasionally, if you complete all your calls in the morning, you can take the afternoon off. Selling permits you to go into a variety of companies and involves you in numerous situations. This kind of schedule is more interesting than working in the same office with the same people, day after day, year after year.

Several Music, Inc.'s distributors say they get very bored sitting in the office. They enjoy calling on accounts.

Number 266 *In most large companies, buyers are very intelligent and conscientious about doing a good job.* It's difficult to con these people into buying a product they don't want or can't use. Generally, they won't make a purchase unless they believe it's a good buy and are interested in long-term relationships with a company or product. In isolated situations, it may be possible to sell a poorly made or unnecessary item. However, in building a long-term business, honesty is important with your customers.

Roy Harrison, the owner of the Seventh Heaven Music Store, is typical of the people Music, Inc.'s sales reps see. He has a Master's Degree in music and is very conscientious.

Additional Sales and Selling Suggestions

Number 267 *Be alert in providing assistance to customers even outside the area of your particular expertise.* In one case, an insurance salesman received additional business from a company because he referred the company to a bank interested in working with small companies. Whenever possible, listen for other problems individuals you are trying to sell may have and try your best to help them.

Music, Inc.'s distributors have been trained to refer customers and music students to the small music stores they deal with.

Number 268 *Don't be a know-it-all, but try to be helpful in a friendly way.* Obviously, you can't solve all a customer's problems, but it's important to show that you care.

Bob Randolph, one of Music, Inc.'s leading distributors, believes that a sale is most likely when a salesperson learns something from a customer and acknowledges it.

Number 269 *Learn a particular buyer's habits so that your calls will be more effective.* For example, there are certain buyers you can call on only Tuesday or Wednesdays. All other times, you will be met with rejections. Obviously, you should avoid calling on these people except on the designated days. Some buyers have a tendency to leave for lunch around 11:30 and come back around 1:30. Others leave at 12:30 and come back around 2:00. If a buyer is rushed at either end of this schedule, you may get a quick brushoff and not have the time you need to show your products. Monday mornings are very difficult because many buyers are really not back into the swing of things with respect to work. The same thing is true of Friday afternoons. Often, buyers are too busy trying to finish up the week's work to see you.

Music, Inc.'s distributors do their administrative reports on Monday mornings and Friday afternoons and concentrate on sales calls the rest of the time

Number 270 *The first time you call on a potential account, arrange an appointment ahead of time.* This applies not only to retail accounts, but to other buyers as well. You can waste considerable time just floating around dropping in on accounts. In some cases, the buyers, especially those for larger stores or accounts, are tied up in meetings and you end up cooling your heels waiting. Occasionally, after you have been able to demonstrate that your products have merit and have found out a particular buyer's habits, it may be possible for you to merely drop by for a talk. However, it is very important in the beginning to have an appointment with the buyers.

When working with small music stores, all sales calls are by appointment.

Number 271 *Being able to write a good business letter often distinguishes you from the competition.* Many salespeople who can write well don't take the time needed to write business letters. They simply feel that letters are not necessary. However, business letters are one of the most effective ways to sell a product or service. Your secretary or sales assistant can type out a letter after you've made a visit to a particular account *or* in some cases, prior to the visit, to introduce you to the account.

The president of Music, Inc. would like his distributors to write introductory and follow-up letters to accounts.

Number 272 *In writing business letters, keep in mind that customers are interested in how you are going to satisfy their needs.* Frankly, customers couldn't care less how qualified you are for your job or how well your company has made other products. They are interested in what you can do for them.

The Music, Inc.'s president stresses the use of "you" in all business letters rather than "I." This procedure focuses attention on the customer's needs.

Number 273 *Often it may take as many as 10 calls and 30 letters before you receive an order from an account.* Try to assess, after the second or third call, how much effort is going to be needed to sell a particular account.

Music, Inc. expects that it will take many sales calls and business letters to get orders from the large music stores.

Number 274 *Informal or formal sales training should be given to every employee of the company.* Employees of any company should understand that everybody, the receptionist, the telephone operator, the secretaries, the warehousemen, the file clerks, and the company president himself or herself, should be friendly to customers and try to be helpful to the people doing the direct selling. The company's existence (and everyone's job) depends on the ability of the employees to sell their products or service to customers.

Music, Inc.'s president has trained his office staff to handle customer phone calls and walk-in requests courteously.

Wishful Thinking vs. Reality

Number 275 *No product will sell itself.* Each product has to be explained and sold to the customer. Even if you have a superior product, it can still take an incredible amount of effort to make a sale. Furthermore, once a product is sold, reorders are seldom automatic. Except in rare cases, you must continue to expend considerable effort to get them. In dealing with most stores, you may have to check the stock of your product on hand and fill out an order form for the buyer to sign. Sometimes reorders require more work than the initial sales. Most of the time, however, the initial sale is the most difficult to make.

Music, Inc.'s machine is new, different, and really has to be demonstrated to justify its price. It very definitely has to be sold.

Number 276 *Do not fall into the trap of assuming that if a particular buyer seems interested in your product and says he will buy it, you will get an immediate order.* A wide variety of events affect the buying of any product. The most important factor is the number of units the buyer has in stock. Perhaps your product is better in quality and lower in price than another. However, there may be a two-year supply of the other item in stock. Once you understand this and make a point to determine when buyers will be placing new orders, you will save yourself much effort. If a buyer cannot place an order right away, frequent sales calls will not help matters. Check back with the buyer in three or four weeks. In the meantime, concentrate on other accounts.

If a buyer purchases one product from your company, do not assume that he will automatically want or need additional products from you. It *is* very useful, if a company buys one product from you, to discuss additional products. However, it is almost always necessary to spend additional time with a buyer explaining those products, if you want them to be considered.

Many music store buyers and owners have expressed an interest in purchasing Music, Inc.'s machine. The company, however, plans to introduce the product slowly and to limit initial sales.

Number 277 *Never assume that your personality will carry a sale.* The truth is that constant follow-up is necessary to be of service to an account. A buyer interested in your personality *only* doesn't last very long.

Although Music, Inc.'s president is an enthusiastic, energetic individual, the ultimate success of the company will depend on the quality of its product and its marketing.

ten

Running the numbers

"Truth is more precious than time."
Disraeli

A real need for a "castle cleaning service" must have existed in the Middle Ages. Castles were not only huge, but dusty, musty, and damp. In addition, knights were forever galloping through the courtyard stirring up dirt. In this chapter, we shall invent just the kind of castle cleaning service that might have thrived to illustrate some important points about running a company.

Number 278 *The only financial statements you need when talking to a bank or another potential investor are an income statement, a balance sheet and a cash-flow statement.* In a more general sense, of course, numerical information is necessary in all areas of small business. In this chapter, we shall talk about the numerical information that is necessary to start a small company. We will discuss sales data, balance-sheet data, income statements, and, also, how to present and interpret cash-flow data. The world increasingly runs on numbers, and you can often legitimize what you are doing with a detailed series of financial statements.

There is a recent statement which some readers may have seen. Two authors once lamented in a *Harvard Business Review* discussion of the financial information received by a company that "the information we want is not the information we need; the information we need is not available." It is next to impossible to run a business well without good numerical data.

Castle Cleaning Incorporated was well equipped with financial data, prepared by its head scribe.

Number 279 *Your breakeven point is your most vital financial statistic.* Above the breakeven point, your firm makes money; below it, your firm loses money. A company's exact breakeven point changes over time; usually it rises faster than you might expect. Knowing what it is at any given moment allows you to judge your performance, even in the crudest possible terms. (If you're above the breakeven point, you're okay; if you're below it, you're not.) A financial analysis book can show you how to prepare a detailed breakeven chart. Most small businesses need only a general breakeven calculation.

Sales Numbers

Number 280 *Always make sure, in calculating sales, that you adjust the numbers by the returns the company receives.* For example, suppose you ship $20,000 worth of merchandise in January and $18,000 worth is returned by a customer dissatisfied with the quality of the merchandise. Your net sales for the month, then, are only $2,000. *Net sales* are gross sales less any returns, allowances, or special discounts offered to customers.

Since Castle Cleaning guarantees satisfaction, unhappy customers may get their money back. The amount returned is subtracted from the monthly sales total.

Number 281 *In certain situations, you may find yourself offering as much as a 10% discount for cash on any particular order.* Make sure that your net sales figures take into account cash discounts. Many decisions in a small company are based on its revenues. It is important to be certain that they are accurately calculated.

Castle Cleaning worked on a cash-only basis. Chickens, sheep, cows, and other barter items were not accepted as payment for the firm's services.

Number 282 *Always be careful about paying freight costs for a customer to protect your margin.* The manager of a small company should review his freight policies frequently. Normally, it costs $18 per 100 pounds to move freight from the West Coast to the East Coast. Freight costs vary as much as $10 per 100 pounds from Los Angeles to Chicago and depend on the commodities being shipped. It is very important not to provide a generous freight allowance unless your profit margins are substantial.

For service firms the cost of getting employees to the worksite is comparable to freight costs. Castle Cleaning always monitored employee travel expenses carefully.

Number 283 *Always give low sales estimates in talking to potential investors or a bank.* That way, you won't be in trouble if the investors or the bank insist that sales reach those levels.

Castle Cleaning estimated its first-year sales at 42 gold pieces (one per castle).

Number 284 *If you are a small company, do not simply add 10% to last year's sales to get a projection of sales for the current year.*

A large company can take last year's sales and add 10% to them to estimate what its sales will be for the current year. For a small company, this procedure is ridiculous for a variety of reasons. Sales may jump 500% in one year if a new customer places a large order. Sales can also decline 50% in one year if the market falls rapidly or several large customers go elsewhere.

One bad job could hurt Castle Cleaning's reputation seriously, since those who owned castles tended to move in the same social circles. Forty-two gold pieces was a conservative estimate of first-year sales.

Number 285 *In estimating total sales for the current year, decide exactly which accounts will place orders and how much they will*

purchase. A sharp banker or potential investor will always look beyond the total sales figure you give him. He will want to know who the accounts are that you're counting on and what they will purchase. You should be prepared for this kind of question. You will be if your own projections are based on this information.

Castle Cleaning estimated that 42 castles would use its services, either weekly, monthly, or once a year.

Number 286 *For any particular market, estimate a penetration rate no higher than 5% if you are a small company.* A large company entering a new market can sometimes get 15% or 20% of it through an intensive marketing effort. A small company entering a new market doesn't have a large enough sales force or advertising budget to make this kind of dent right away. In some cases, a small company with the best product in a particular market will only sell 1% to 2% of that market. Moreover, even if it had been able to sell 15% of the market, a small company might not have had the resources to produce that large a volume of merchandise.

The president of Castle Cleaning estimated that there were 840 castles in the country. His first-year goal was to clean 5% of them, or 42 castles.

Number 287 *In projecting sales, determine what sales mix you expect to have, whether there will be several large accounts, if there is any seasonality to the large accounts' orders, and how you will approach the accounts to determine future sales.* Sales estimates are the first step in projecting your income for a period. If you start off badly with a wrong assumption about sales, no amount of slashing away at overhead will be very effective in reducing your losses.

Castle Cleaning had one rate for castles with over 10 rooms, another rate for castles with over 20 rooms, and a deluxe rate for castles with over 30 rooms. It expected each type of castle to provide one-third of its first-year total business.

Income Statements

Number 288 *Income statements should always be rounded off to the nearest dollar.* Too much time can be wasted trying to make an income statement agree to the last nickel with the retained earnings figure on your balance sheet. It is often very difficult to get these two figures to balance in any event, and it is especially hard if you are not working with round dollar amounts. An *income statement* is a tool for calculating your profit or loss. Being able to read and write income statements quickly is a valuable skill for anyone running a small business, since they are likely to be required by investors and banks as well as state and federal tax offices.

Castle Cleaning Incorporated's income statements were rounded off to the nearest dollar.

Number 289 *In preparing an income statement, always include once-a-year expenses such as local inventory taxes.* Taxes have increased in many states to more than half a firm's profits. For example, in California, 60% of profits over $50,000 may be paid in taxes.

Castle Cleaning paid a special business tax to the king, which it included on its income statements.

Number 290 *Remember, too, that under the new federal tax law, profits up to $50,000 are taxed at 21% and those over $50,000 are taxed at 48%.* (The first $25,000 is taxed at 20% and the second $25,000 at 22%; hence the average tax on the first $50,000 of 21%.) State and local taxes must also be calculated using up-to-date rates.

The scribe for Castle Cleaning used the latest tax rate in drawing up its income statement.

Balance Sheets

Number 291 *Think of a balance sheet in terms of what you own (the firm's assets), what you owe (its liabilities), and the money that stockholders have put into the company (its net worth).* All this can be combined into a basic accounting equation anyone running his or her own business should understand: Assets = liabilities + net worth. Balance-sheet data like that on an income statement should be rounded to the nearest dollar. Don't waste your time calculating assets and liabilities to the last cent.

Castle Cleaning's president understood the basic accounting equation very well.

Number 292 *Be prepared to have potential investors and bankers comment on the balance sheet's current ratio.* A firm's current ratio is simply its current assets divided by its current liabilities. If this ratio is less than one, the condition of the company is considered to be not very good. If it is 1.5 or higher, the company owns considerably more than it owes and should be fairly well off. Current assets are important because they can be quickly converted into cash to pay debts.

Castle Cleaning, with a current ratio of 2, appeared to be in good shape.

Number 293 *Be aware that there is a variety of possibilities for handling product development costs on a balance sheet.* Certain companies have large expenditures for product development. These are expenses that may be spread (or *capitalized*) over a period of five years. For example, you may spend $100,000 on product development in 1980, but show only $20,000 in expenses. The other $80,000 then appears on the balance sheet as an asset. The rationale for spreading out product development costs in this way is that, although the money is spent in one year, the benefits from it are spread out over a period of five years. Doing it may be very misleading, however, because it makes a firm look like it has a stronger current ratio than it really does.

The cost of developing equipment (long-handled brooms and dustmops) for Castle Cleaning was spread over five years.

Number 294 *If you have high profits in a particular year, you should expense all your product development costs.* If you use your product development costs to offset your high profits, your taxable income will be reduced. Usually, in a new, small company there are initial losses. The choice is usually between writing off one-fifth of the product development costs in the current year and looking better to potential investors or writing them all off one year to generate a tax loss for the following year.

Castle Cleaners expected to expense its product development costs in its third year.

Number 295 *It is important for an entrepreneur to learn as much as possible about financial statements.* Your accountant can help you here. So can a very good booklet available from the world's largest securities firm, Merrill Lynch Pierce Fenner & Smith. This 24-page red book, entitled "Understanding Financial Statements," is so good that it is often handed out in graduate-level finance courses. It discusses balance sheets, cash-flow statement, and profit and loss statements. You can obtain a copy by calling or writing your local Merrill Lynch office.

Sir Hilary Higgins, Castle Cleaning's president, studied and was familiar with financial statements.

Cash Flows

Number 296 *Never expect that most of your customers will pay their bills in 30 days.* This is especially true if you are dealing with small accounts. Many small companies are started with inadequate financing and find it difficult to pay their bills within even 60 days. You should assume that 50% to 60% of your accounts (if you are dealing with small accounts) will pay within 30 to 45 days. Another 30 or 40% will probably pay within 60 days, and 10% in 90 days. Probably 3% will never pay at all. These numbers should be reflected in your sales and financial statements.

By asking for cash immediately upon completion of a job, Castle Cleaners hopes to avoid nonpayment problems.

Number 297 *Never assume that inventory will replenish itself.* Often in preparing a cash-flow statement, an individual forgets he must occasionally replenish his inventory and pay the suppliers. Always check your inventory flows.

The principal resource of Castle Cleaning is its inventory of cleaning supplies.

Number 298 *For simplicity, view a cash-flow statement as a statement of the sum of the inflows and outflows of cash into the company and their net effect.* You should be aware that the day after you finish preparing the cash-flow statement, changes in your cash position will have already occurred. You will have made several expenditures and incurred additional expenses. Dollars will have flowed in and out of the company. Don't be surprised, therefore, if banks or investors question you about these changes when you secure financing.

Castle Cleaning's inflows will be the payments from castle owners for its services. Its outflows will be wages for its employees and payments for cleaning supplies and equipment.

Number 299 *Occasionally, you will meet someone—probably a banker—who says he or she doesn't believe in cash-flow statements.* A good way to answer this is to say that cash-flow statements are merely a management guide. It is difficult for a small company to estimate when accounts will pay their bills, but the information is needed. It will help you to determine when to buy merchandise, when to borrow from the bank, and when you will have cash available for product development. If your company is well capitalized (and most aren't), then a cash-flow statement won't be as important to you because you'll be able to pay your bills on time even if accounts are delinquent.

Brother Wilber, the monk in charge of Castle Cleaning account with the Medieval Bank, is a great believer in cash-flow statements.

Number 300 *You should prepare cash-flow statements monthly, unless funds are so short that you need to monitor cash flows weekly or daily.* Most banks, potential investors, and stockholders require monthly reports.

Because of Brother Wilber's interest in cash flows, Castle Cleaning Incorporated prepares weekly cash-flow statements.

Adjustments

Number 301 *If your financial statements are for the IRS and your objective is to minimize taxes, you are going to have to make several choices with respect to inventory evaluation and capitalization.* Normally, if your company has suffered a series of losses over the first two years, you will want to do everything within legal limits to make your statements look as good as possible and the losses as small as possible.

Castle Cleaning's scribe was familiar with medieval tax regulations.

Number 302 *With respect to inventory, you will have to choose whether to use the Fifo (first in, first out) or the Lifo (last in, first out) method of valuation.* This decision is very important, because once you choose, you must be consistent or prepare a large number of additional forms. In a period when prices are rising dramatically, it may be important to use the Fifo system. This will result in a higher profit figure. However, because you have had to pay more for the merchandise still in stock, the value of your inventory will also be higher than it would be using another method. If you use the Lifo system, your profits will be lower and so will the value of your inventory, since the more expensive last items in will have been the first items out. Your accountant will draw up your financial statements. Your responsibility is to determine which method of inventory valuation he or she will use.

Because cleaning supplies (Castle Cleaning's inventory) had to be brought in on horseback, the firm used the normally higher-cost Lifo method of inventory valuation.

Number 303 *In considering whether to capitalize product development costs, you must decide if you will spread them over five years.* If you expense them (write them off entirely in the current year), this will obviously increase your expenses and thereby lower your profits or increase your losses. Early capitalization decisions are important because they may limit your options in future years.

Castle Cleaners will write off certain expenses for small tools such as rakes, scrapers, and shovels in one year.

General Budgeting Suggestions

Number 304 *If your accountant or bookkeeper is unable to produce detailed financial reports in response to requests for information, consider preparing summary reports.* When a company is new, there is generally pressure from the bank and from investors for information on the firm's operations. "Where are your financial data?" is the common cry. Summary reports based on the best information you have will get a much better reception than no reports at all.

Castle Cleaning's president draws up short profit and loss summaries weekly.

Number 305   *To protect yourself against accusations that reports have been prepared from inaccurate data, type the word "unaudited" at the top of any reports you prepare yourself.* Occasionally, you will hear people use the phrase "To the best of my knowledge, the information is correct." This puts the speaker under no obligation to verify the information and in fact implies that it may not be entirely accurate. Similarly the word "unaudited" on a financial report indicates that some of the numbers may change at a future date when more precise information becomes available from the accountants.

Castle Cleaning's weekly profit and loss statements have "unaudited" written at the top.

Number 306   *Every manager of a new company should learn how to estimate financial statements.* It is helpful to have the general outline of financial statements in your mind so that you can, when necessary, make up estimated statements quickly. The following table is a rough guide to calculating particular items that usually appear on financial reports:

Cost of goods sold	60% of sales
Gross margin	40% of sales
Expenses (overhead)	25% of sales
Net margin	15% of sales
Taxes	50% of net margin
Net profit	7½% of sales

Learning how to estimate these items helps you to run

spot checks on your financial position and attack problems before they get too large to handle. If you find, for example, that your overhead expenses are substantially higher than 25% of your sales, you should take immediate action and not wait for formal financial statements to tell you that you are in hot water.

Castle Cleaning Incorporated's president is an expert at estimating financial statements.

Number 307 *It is of the utmost importance for a firm's manager to develop a feel for financial problems and quickly stop erosion in any particular area.* Estimating is the quickest way to find problems before they become obvious.

Castle Cleaning's president's skill at estimating has helped identify several problem areas for the firm.

Number 308 *It is always helpful to have several professional advisors who can assist you if you get in financial trouble.* A good accountant, preferably a CPA, who can assist and advise you is invaluable. It is also important to have an attorney who is knowledgeable about financial matters. A junior partner in a law firm would be particularly helpful to know and would probably be more helpful to a small company than a senior partner whose time was at a premium.

Haskell Stevens, a junior partner in the firm of Merlin and Nimue, has been advising Castle Cleaning about its finances.

Number 309 *Never get so carried away working with numbers that you forget your main job of making and marketing products.* Financial reports are essentially a way of keeping score for the company. Like a score card in a baseball game, they don't tell you everything about the quality of the play.

Castle Cleaning was aware of this possible problem.

Number 310 *A second big mistake is to assume that the present* *and future history of a company will be exactly the same as the past.* It is important to remember that financial statements represent the operations of the company in the past. The present is never exactly the same as the past, and a manager's judgment is of critical importance in assessing the risk associated with present and future operations.

Castle Cleaning's president prided himself on being prepared for the unexpected.

Number 311 *It is also a mistake for the board of directors to try to figure out and make decisions about the future of the company solely on the basis of data on past operations.* Particularly since the board of directors is less involved in the operations of the company. Many misleading decisions can be made based on past company history. The manager of a small company should strive to educate its directors to make decisions based on future expectations about the marketplace and products.

Castle Cleaning's board includes several castle owners and royal ministers. They have been educated by the company's president to look to future market possibilities when making decisions.

eleven

Finding, selling, and filling the big order

"To climb steep hills requires a slow pace at first."

Shakespeare

With the secret entry of many companies into the cosmetics business it seems only natural to wonder what great works Venus, the Roman goddess of love, could have done with a line of her own cosmetics. In this chapter, we shall see how Venus Cosmetics, Inc. might have turned out.

Number 312 *It is unrealistic for a new, small company to plan on getting an order from one of the 500 largest companies listed in* FORTUNE *magazine.* However, it is helpful while you are developing a base of small customers to be aware of what larger companies are doing. You may have a chance eventually to find, sell, and fill a big order. By a large order, we mean either something that will at least double the size of your company and/or maybe even make it 10 times as large as its current size. There is a variety of risks associated with going after an order that will increase your size dramatically. There is also a variety of rewards, which will be discussed later in the chapter.

Venus Cosmetics planned to start small and only look for large orders in three years.

Number 313 *Besides increasing your revenues, a large order from a large company would legitimize your company and your products.* Once another company or your banker hears that you are selling products to Sears Roebuck or General Motors, you should have no problem increasing your capitalization.

Venus hoped eventually to sell the distributor who supplies all the Roman gods. Her cosmetics would then be used throughout the land.

Finding the Big Order

Number 314 *To establish yourself with a large company requires a special set of circumstances. Look for a change in the business and economic environment to give you a chance to be heard.* A new small company, unless its product is very unusual, will have a hard time cracking the resistance of a large company. Good business relationships are built over 15 or 20 years, and it is very hard to displace a traditional supplier or product. Look for a substantial change in the business environment to help you. Where there is a change, an opportunity may exist for establishing yourself or filling a need. Sometimes such a change can be the result of new laws or regulations. Several companies in the computer business benefited considerably from the regulations and laws that were changed in 1970 and 1971. Also, several local telephone companies were given a substantial boost when it was ruled that they could buy their supplies from outside contractors rather than the General Telephone Company. While it's true that changes in business and economic conditions may cause a certain amount of upheaval and inconvenience, they may also create unique opportunities for enterprising firms.

Venus believed her company would be successful because the Roman gods were tired of war and ready for love.

Number 315 *Skim business magazines for information that may be valuable to your industry.* It is impossible to keep up with everything that occurs in the business world. However, it is an excellent idea to make reading three business magazines, *Business Week, Forbes,* and *Fortune,* part of the normal routine of your life. The information, in *Business Week,* that a large company was going to move into a new area led one very small company (after 1½ years of effort) to a half-a-million-dollar sales contract. There is obviously no guarantee that finding something out in one of these magazines will help your company. There is also no guarantee that you will be the only one to try to make use of the information. However, the magazines may stimulate you to think of something new and profitable for your firm to try.

Very few business magazines existed in Venus's day.

Number 316 *One way of finding out about a large potential order is through the Small Business Administration's export service.* As we mentioned in Chapter 8, the SBA will provide any company that registers with it a list of overseas companies who are looking for suppliers in the United States. Although this service doesn't usually generate large orders, there are situations where special suppliers are needed. For example, the newfound wealth of the Middle East has led to several requests for large amounts of merchandise for that area in recent years.

Number 317 *The normal course of business may produce several possibilities of large orders.* Simply attending trade shows and contacting accounts may produce some large orders or some new ideas for ways to get large orders.

Venus planned to collect export data with a view to marketing her new line of cosmetics to several Greek gods.

Selling the Big Order

Number 318 *Especially in selling a big order, timing is of critical importance.* Just as timing is important in starting a company (it's a lot easier when money is plentiful), so too timing is important in looking for a large order. It's easier to get when the potential buyer is expanding.

Venus expected to have no trouble getting a large order, since the use of cosmetics was becoming more popular.

Number 319 *For many companies, it may take five years to develop a new area of business.* It may even take 15 years. This can be discouraging to the manager of a small company who wishes to sell his or her products and is under pressure to produce earnings quickly. The simple reality of the marketplace is that many large orders take a long time to get.

Venus spent five years studying formulas for cosmetics before evolving the formula for Quiver, her perfume for goddesses.

Number 320 *Ask yourself the following questions to determine whether a large company is seriously interested in developing a new program in which your company's products can play a role.*

1. Have they developed similar programs in the past?
2. How long did it take them to develop those other programs?
3. How successful were those programs?
4. How interested are the personnel involved in the new program in expansion?

5. If the program is unsuccessful, will the managers of the program be likely to lose their jobs?
6. Does the company have a schedule for the new program?
7. Can your company afford to wait while the program is being developed?
8. Is the amount of time it's going to take to get the new order economical for you?

All these questions need to be asked to give yourself a better feel for whether your efforts will be rewarded.

The major distributor for the Roman gods met all the tests set up by the questions. Venus felt she had a good chance for a large order from him.

Number 321 *In working with a large company, the theme for your overall approach should be "anything to help the buyer."* Usually the buyer or purchasing agent for a large company is under a substantial amount of pressure. This is especially true if a program is new and he or she may be out of a job if it goes badly. Try to help the buyer in every way you can, particularly if you are trying to sell a large order. Try being creative and providing things the buyer needs, such as schedules and outlines.

Bacchus, the Roman god of wine, fertility, and wild behavior was the chief buyer for the other gods. Venus had a good relationship with him and planned to give him an outline for placing orders.

Number 322 *Remember that summaries are very helpful to buyers.* Buyers can be snowed under by product information from a company, and most are very receptive to a summary of information. It is useful, if you are going to present a formal proposal, to make the top page the summary page.

Venus planned to give Bacchus a summary of her products.

Number 323 *Telephone buyers frequently.* If buyers are nearby, it should be easy to visit their offices. In most cases they are in another city. It is helpful, then, to call them every two to four days to check what is happening on a project. If necessary, invent a reason for calling or asking a question.

Venus talked with Bacchus every two to three days.

Number 324 *Send the buyers for large projects any market-research information you come upon that is relevant to your industry and their projects.* Often the market research department of a large company will develop the information needed for a special program or service. However, it never hurts to make sure that the buyers for such programs are informed about what is happening in the marketplace. They may be too busy talking to various suppliers to keep abreast of who is buying what and what products are moving well.

Venus gave Bacchus a market research report prepared by Concept Surveys Inc. which showed that the Roman people, as well as the gods, were ready for cosmetics especially Quiver perfume.

Number 325 *Provide buyers with industry information.* By being in an industry you can find out what other industry suppliers are doing and use this information to your advantage. For example, if you are selling safety equipment and 3M or Monsanto has come up with a new reflective material that can be sewn on your products, this information should be passed on to your accounts.

Bacchus was also interested in what Greek cosmeticians were doing.

Number 326 *Make sure you offer your products as private-label products for large accounts.* Unfortunately for many small businesses, the economic influence in their industry is being increasingly concentrated in a small number of very large companies. Because the financial power of these companies helps them dominate the advertising and marketing of that industry, their brand names become well established. On the other hand, many of the large retailers, supermarket chains, and commercial buyers use a substantial amount of private-label products to increase their profits. This creates a very good situation for small companies who do not have the money to advertise widely and wish to offer their products to a large retailer or commercial account. The private-label strategy is not recommended for everyone, since you are essentially helping the commercial account build their own name. However, a private-label arrangement should not disturb your ordinary marketing relationships, since you are not selling your own brand through the same retail, discount, or commercial outlets.

Venus offered Cupid, the Roman god of love, his own private label since she expected him to be a large buyer.

Number 327 *Never push or strong-arm a buyer verbally.* If buyers make comments such as "Let me call you once or twice" or are fairly quick to end a telephone conversation with you, maybe you are pressuring them too much. Try instead to adapt an attitude of being always helpful, always available.

Venus adopted an easy going, low-key approach to selling that was natural to her.

The Company Visit

Number 328 *As part of the sales of any large order, you should expect the buyer and his or her associates to visit your company.* It is easy for a small company to panic at the thought of being surveyed in detail by the buyer of a large company. However, usually unless you absolutely fall flat on your face the order will not be decided on the basis of the company visit. Often the individuals coming to visit simply want to make sure that the company exists (that it has offices and a staff).

Many people in the aerospace industry may be aware of a Los Angeles company that started doing business in the manager's garage. All of a sudden, the Department of Defense telephoned to say that six staff members would be out in two days to visit the company plant, talk to the personnel, and inspect the facilities.

The manager immediately went out and rented a warehouse and a large amount of equipment and hired his family and relatives as a staff. By working all night, a sign painter painted several signs with the company name and a description of the product inside the plants. When the Department of Defense people arrived, they saw that the company was very new, but did have a warehouse, equipment, and staff. Ultimately an order worth several hundred thousand dollars was placed with the firm.

Many people believe in a company that has equipment and facilities (although these companies go out of business as easily as those without equipment and large warehouses). Occasionally, you'll need to prepare to show your best side to buyers from large companies.

Venus fully expected Bacchus and his assistant buyers to visit her cosmetics manufacturing facility. She believed they would be impressed.

Filling the Big Order

Number 329 *It should not come as a surprise to the manager of a small company that even with a large order in hand he has difficulty raising the funds he needs to fill it.* A small company may be viewed by investors as unable to handle a large order it has received.

Venus expected to have to spend considerable time getting additional financing if Bacchus gave her a large order.

Number 330 *Often it may be necessary to get the company buying merchandise from a small company to guarantee the order, or even to pledge the order to a bank, to secure the funds needed to fill the order.* Pledging the order to the bank is a very effective way to ensure that the bank is involved in the company and its operations.

Some Roman gods helped Venus by guaranteeing their orders.

Number 331 *Getting three quotes on all purchases is mandatory.* As we have already discussed, you should never simply rely on the first quote from one supplier for merchandise. Although it is easier and sometimes a lazy man's way to get by on the first quote because it sounds right, three quotes are of value on every large purchase of products or components. Many times these quotes can be obtained over the phone so it is not necessary to write letters.

Venus always got three quotes on compounds used in her products.

Number 332 *Discuss any changes, however small, in a large order with the buyer.* A small company should never make changes in a design or a product for a particular large order without discussing it with the buyer.

Bacchus was kept appraised of all Venus's product changes.

Number 333 *Large purchases may be advisable even if the merchandise must be held for six months.* In some businesses, such as the greeting-card business, it is useful to buy in large quantities and hold the merchandise for as long as six to eight months. This makes for more economical, longer production runs.

Venus concluded that in making cosmetics she should purchase various compounds in large quantities.

Number 334 *With respect to printing materials, try to run several items at once.* Substantial savings can be made by running two, four, six, or even eight printed items at once, since this saves set-up time for the printer. You may be able to save as much as 30% this way.

All printed materials for Venus Cosmetics were given to the scribes at once.

Number 335 *Provide honest, realistic delivery dates.* Buyers always want to know when their orders will be delivered. Even though there may be some grumbling initially, in the long run you will benefit from giving a realistic delivery date. In fact, it is very helpful to add some extra time as a cushion for the usual delays.

Number 336 *Discussing partial delivery with a large account may be very valuable.* If it is not possible to deliver a full order as of a certain date, determine whether the buyer will accept partial delivery. Knowing that at least some of the merchandise has been shipped may quiet the account and allow you to work on the rest of the order with peace of mind.

Bacchus's large orders for Venus's cosmetics were to be handled by making partial deliveries. All the Quiver Perfume manufactured was to be sent directly to Bacchus.

twelve

A review of the first year and some key conclusions

"It is easy to be wise after the fact."
English proverb

Even if you carefully follow every suggestion in this book, luck and timing are important in the development of a new business. It is also crucial that the new company's managers be survivors, capable of working effectively under pressure.

Managers must be able to shift gears quickly. If their company manufactures artificial sweeteners and the Food and Drug Administration suddenly bans them, they must be able to come up with an alternate product or expand other areas of their business. Since you can't control everything, survival requires flexibility.

The fast-changing business environment makes frequent reviews of company strategy important. To keep the year-end review brief, we have first described what you will usually discover at the end of the first year and then consolidate our advice into key suggestions for each functional area.

Reviewing the First Year

At the end of the first 12 months, most new companies show some signs of life. However, they have usually spent more money than they planned, called on fewer customers, and developed fewer products. On the other hand, the managers have learned a few things and, it is hoped, are a lot better prepared for the second year.

During the first year, almost every new company makes a series of discoveries:

Number 337 *Probably the most important thing a new company finds out is that it needs a stronger, more unique product line.* Normally a company is started without the manager's knowing in detail what the competition is doing or planning. It's pretty shocking to find out that a competitor has done exactly what you have done, or plans to introduce a product that is superior to yours. At the end of the first year, you need to make a painful assessment of the worth and marketability of your product line.

Number 337A *New companies also learn that they must be in a position of selling something extra.* They have to be unique in some way. There has to be something different, some new wrinkle, about their approach to marketing and product development. Review the uniqueness of your marketing strategies and your product line closely at the close of the first twelve months.

Number 338 *At the end of the first year, a new company usually finds that it needs stronger financing.* Larger bank loans and more equity capital are usually required. The company needs to strengthen its ties with individual investors interested in the firm's survival.

Number 339 *If it has done a considerable amount of business in its first year, a new company usually finds that its internal systems are a disaster.* Its methods of handling orders, invoices, credit, and bookkeeping may all need to be improved. On the other hand, if the company does very little business, the managers may find out that they have oversystemized and overorganized some tasks.

Number 340 *At the end of the first year, a company usually finds that it must strengthen its marketing effort.* It must improve its sales force, its advertising, and its market research.

In spite of all the arguments that starting a new company is best done in a logical and well-reasoned way, beginning a new company is an emotional challenge. The effort involved stresses and stretches an individual's mind. As a result, the founder usually makes the following personal discoveries:

Number 341 *A detached viewpoint, an ability to not become totally involved emotionally, keeps the ulcers away.* A very emotional involvement in a company may be helpful for a short period of time. However, total emotional involvement in a sustained effort to develop a company may be detrimental to both you and the firm. Decisions based on emotion are, more times than not, hasty and ill-advised. Get involved, but not totally. Keep some emotional distance.

Number 342 *There are always days when you won't feel like doing certain things.* On some days calling back someone who has called you or arguing with a consumer or supplier may be a chore. On those days, it is best to do the things you don't want to do first, if they must be done, and after that, it is hoped, the day will be easier.

Number 343 *It's essential to avoid creeping apathy because your company is still an also ran in the marketplace.* Too many turndowns can make you want to adopt the slogan, "We're Number 3 . . . why should we try at all?" This attitude will make it impossible to come up with the new ideas you need to turn your company around. Try taking a walk, talking to a friend—anything to get your mind reoriented to being creative and developing a unique company.

In assessing the first year, demonstrating early successes is important. This helps suppliers have confidence in you, stockholders remain quiet, the bank extend additional loans, and employees develop confidence in the company. If a product is selling well or you have captured a key account, credit and funds will be easier to secure.

In assessing the first year, any new company will find dollars wasted. There will be some overhead expenses that weren't planned. Some products will bomb in the market! Some market tests will be unsuccessful. You should be spending only a small amount of money on each product that didn't work. You will always find out that half your advertising dollars were wasted. The question is which half?

Time is money, and in reviewing the first year you will find considerable nonproductive effort. You'll also find that considerable time was spent on marginal products.

Number 344 *If your company was in a short or tight cash position during the first year, prepare general cash-flow statements and other financial statements every several days to help you understand where the business stands and plan how the business will develop.*

Some Key Conclusions

MARKETING

Number 345 *In marketing, persistence pays off.* However, there are certain limits. If there is no hope at all that an account either needs your product or will ever buy it, stop wasting your time contacting the account.

Number 346 *Always gear your goods to the customer's needs, using such words as "you may need" or "it might be in your interest."*

Number 347 *Be truthful.* Statements like "We don't happen to carry it, but we can get it for you" will win you more dollars in the long run by showing your account that you are (a) truthful and (b) interested in helping them out.

Number 348 *Keep to your schedule and meet deadlines.* If you tell a customer that merchandise will be delivered as of a certain date, make sure you deliver it by that date.

Number 349 *Respond to your customers' comments before offering your own.* Give credit to his or her suggestions, ideas, and objections to your products.

Number 350 *Bring out a product's special benefits for your customers.* Don't confuse them with details during the first interview. Concentrate on establishing the three or four special benefits of your product or service.

Number 351 *Send your major customers a mailing or other literature once a month.* Give them a new product idea or a different merchandising approach, something that will keep them interested in your company. They will be pleased to have received the mailing and do business with you.

Number 352 *Give press releases to specialized trade magazines to save advertising dollars.*

Number 353 *If you're selling consumer products, make store audits once every two weeks.* Carefully check the price and quality of goods, new products from competitors, and how individual stores are doing. If you are selling a service, visit clients who have used your service in the past to find out how they are doing.

Number 354 *Use business letters as a selling tool and as a follow-up to important sales calls.*

PRODUCTION

Number 355 *Add two additional weeks to any normal schedule to shakedown and debug new machines or tooling.*

Number 356 *Specify exactly the grade and hardness of steel to be used in any steel product.*

Number 357 *Remember that estimates of the amount of a product used each month are very helpful in projecting sales and also in ordering.*

Number 358 *Be aware that, in the production area, it takes 30 days to breathe.* It is very, very difficult to get anything going in 30 days. People need time to act to your ideas and plans.

Number 359 *Remember that production standards, even approximate ones, are almost always more helpful than saying "here's a job—see how many of these you can do" or "we'd like to have you work in this area."*

Number 360 *Find out what your production people need, and want, and then do your best to provide it.*

FINANCE

Number 361 *When money is tight, always conserve cash.* Although spending for new product development and advertising is important, see if, through innovative thinking, you can cut back on expenditures in both these areas. Some people will argue that when money is tight, more advertising is needed. However, possibly more public relations and more personal calls by the top executives of the company on newspaper or magazine editors would be more useful than more advertising.

Number 362 *In a seasonal business, purchase distressed inventory at the end of one season, and carry it over to the next season.* This can be extremely helpful in increasing your margins since merchandise is often sold at the end of one season for prices at which it is impossible to buy it at the start of the next season. However, the benefits should be carefully weighed against the interest paid on the purchase money.

Number 363 *Calculate that 60% of your customers will pay on time or sooner, 30% will pay one or two months late, and 10% will be very difficult to get your money from.* The larger the customer's company, the easier it is to get them to pay their bills. Plan your cash flow and cash needs accordingly.

Number 364 *Remember that many companies fail because of undercapitalization, even though they had a good idea.* Make sure you have enough financing for your company. If anything, try to get more capital than you actually think you will need. (This is easier said then done, of course!)

DEALING WITH BANKS

Number 365 *Never make an initial visit to a bank without a balance sheet, an income statement, and a cash-flow statement.*

Number 366 *Always send your banker information once a month.* Discuss the company's progress and plans with him or her once a month via the telephone. Stop by at the bank occasionally rather than always having the banker meet you in your office.

Number 367 *Remember that a bank will always look at a company's equity position in evaluating it.* That's the position that comes after the bank if any of the company's assets must be liquidated.

Number 368 *Always try to give the bank some idea of what might happen if certain problems were encountered in the course of doing business.*

Number 369 *Never scare a bank or a banker with special problems. If they affect the financial position of the company, simply advise the bank well in advance through letter or a telephone call.* Remember, bankers are used to problems and problem companies.

DEALING WITH STOCKHOLDERS

Number 370 *Remember that stockholders are primarily concerned with two things: putting up more money and dilution of the stock.* Everything else, including new products, special customers you're calling on, taxes you have to pay, problems with your employees, and problems with your spouse, is of much less interest to them (unless, of course, these things affect whether they have to put up more money or suffer dilution).

Number 371 *Send stockholder information out once a month. Determine what information your stockholders would like at an annual meeting.*

Number 372 *Have stockholders meet one another at lunch or in company work sessions.* Being part of a group gives people confidence, and if one investor loses his money, he will feel there are people who can commiserate with him.

ADMINISTRATION

Number 373 *Hire people with multiple skills.* It's far better to pay $900 a month for a secretary/bookkeeper than pay two employees $600 a month to do the same work.

Number 374 *Give frequent raises, even if they're small.* This lets the members of your staff know that you are thinking about them and doing the best you can for them. Also, comment that you are not able to give them as much money as you would like.

Number 375 *Spend a little time with each employee every day.* This does not necessarily mean you have to praise each employee. By spending a little time with people you let them know that you are interested in their welfare.

Number 376 *If a particular individual seems to be slowing down or lacking motivation, occasionally work directly with that individual on a special project.*

Number 377 *Remember that titles are important.* Wherever possible, give people titles that will be useful in their dealings with customers and suppliers. These people would rather see an office manager than a receptionist. If there's only one clerical/secretarial employee in your office, why not give this person the title of office manager?

PURCHASING

Number 378 *In working on a key project, figure out which of the important components or subassemblies takes the longest time to get, and concentrate on securing that item.* If you're pressed for time, you can allow other products to slide. A mistake in the component with the longer lead time, however, adds to the overall length of the project. (For sophisticated projects a scheduling chart can be used.)

Number 379 *Always have two sources for critical items.* This way, if suppliers are tight you can still be fairly sure of supplying your customers.

Number 380 *In making large purchases, never deal with just one supplier.* Even though the product may not be critical, you will get a better deal by using two suppliers rather than one.

Number 381 *Always use purchase-order forms.* This will give you a record of what you ordered and save time when ordering similar items.

Number 382 *Always obtain three quotes on a product or service.* You will find that there is a wide variety in what people will charge you. For example, one firm that needed the outside of its warehouse painted received some quotes that were three times as high as the contract it eventually signed.

Number 383 *Often a detailed specification sheet will get you much lower quotes than a general specification sheet.* If you supply details, suppliers know exactly what you want. If they have to estimate, or be able to rely on certain materials, then they will be forced to quote you a high price to have an acceptable margin of error.

THE USE OF TIME

Number 384 *Always telephone before going anywhere important.* This, obviously, saves time and gas mileage.

Number 385 *Always have an appointment for a sales call.* Nothing is more frustrating than to show up and find out that the buyer you wanted to call on is out of town, has suddenly been called away, or has decided to take the afternoon off to play golf.

Number 386 *Make lists.* This forces you to set priorities and brings into perspective what you have to do. You can then tackle your problems in a rational manner.

Number 387 *If there is too much to do, always do whatever will bring in the most cash first.* Think of business in terms of the cash it produces.

Number 388 *Limit appointments and meetings to one hour.* Strong arguments for longer meetings are made by many people. However, even in dealing with important problems that will take longer than an hour to solve, it's usually helpful to take an hour's crack at them, then come back to them later.

Number 389 *Learn to estimate important variables like sales by calculating them frequently in your head rather than spending all your time on long, detailed analyses.* Sales projections are vital and should be estimated *monthly.*

Number 390 *Once you've accepted an insurance plan, don't waste time constantly reviewing it or seeing insurance agents.* Establish an insurance plan and review it only once every three years. Your time is too valuable to be wasted talking to insurance people, except to ask an occasional question.

Number 391 *Before meeting with anyone who wants to sell you something, ask them to send you a letter describing the product. This will give you a chance to learn something about the products before the meeting.* Often people will send information to you and you can get back to them with questions. Maybe a meeting isn't even necessary, though normally you will need additional information. In this way, you can actually speed up the decision process.

PLANNING

Number 392 *Have a contingency plan for the company if events don't work out in your favor.*

Number 393 *Develop an overall goal for the company.* An overall goal rallies employees, stockholders, and financial people to support the firm.

Number 394 *Always have a plan for your own personal future if your company goes bankrupt.* You should figure this out even to the point of updating your résumé from time to time in case you need to cut your losses and look for a job.

Number 395 *What your company will do depends on the needs of your customers.* Consider your customers and their needs carefully in preparing a general business plan. In fact, it's often important to pretest your ideas on your customers before you develop a plan or a marketing approach.

SETTING UP A BOARD OF DIRECTORS

Number 396 *In a small company the board of directors is usually made up of the company manager, his or her spouse, and the attorney for the company.* Normally this works quite well when the company is just starting out. There is no need to set up a formal board of directors.

Number 397 *Once the company has over $250,000 in annual sales, you should develop a more formal five- or seven-person board of directors.*

Number 398 *It is important to remember than an outside board of directors does not, repeat, does not know the business.* The best use of outside directors is as a source of contacts and to establish a regular reporting system for the managers of the company.

Number 399 *Don't load the board of directors with friends only.* Always have one or two outside directors who will raise questions and provide different viewpoints. You don't need a constant repetition of what is standard company thinking.

SURVIVING

Number 400 *The chief goal of any corporation in the first year, and probably for longer than that, is to survive.* Unless you are blessed with an abundance of capital, it is important that the company establish a solid base for survival during the first year.

Number 401 *In order to survive you must have products and you must have customers.* Constantly review what you have done to develop good products and secure customers.

Number 402 *Unless you are in a very unique business, you will need to rely heavily on other people in the organization.* Instead of having a detailed hierarchy, try to develop a small, efficient working team that is knowledgeable about most company activities.

Conclusion

In the end, you're on your own as far as decisions with respect to your company are concerned. Suggestions can be offered by numerous people—by suppliers, by outside assistants and others—but the final decisions are yours.

It is very important to develop judgment, or a feel for the company so that you know where to spend your time and which sections of the business need your attention. Usually what happens is that one out of ten projects will succeed; therefore, it's important to get ten projects rolling, not to spend a lot on money on them, but at least get them off the ground.

Usually five years are needed to develop a substantial company. The first year is essentially a year of surviving. The second year is a year of some market success. The third is a year of building upon the base of the first two years. The fourth is a year of making some money, and the fifth is one in which you are well established. Obviously this is not true in every case or in every industry, but it's best to figure on a five-year effort to establish yourself. There are only rare instances of fast millions being accumulated.

With luck, alertness, creativity, and persistence, you may be able one day to tell your grandchildren, "I created a successful company." All the effort will then have been worthwhile, and the personal satisfaction you feel may be more of a reward than dollars and cents.

Number 403 *Anything well planned will not quite work out as you well planned.* Just notice that Fox and Mancuso planned on 402 things, and, rather than change the number to 403, cheated a little and didn't renumber. However, if you caught this error, you may well be on your way—so, good luck.

Appendixes

A. Sources of Equity Funding for a New Company

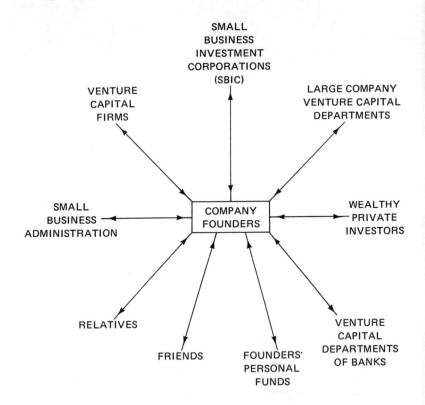

B. Bankruptcy

Bankruptcy is a process created by law to solve in a fair way the interest of both the creditor who is owed the money and the debtor who is not able to pay his debts. In 1978 President Carter signed a major amendment to the bankruptcy law, and bankruptcy laws have changed dramatically. The changes were all fundamental improvements. Although it may be depressing to have a section of this appendix entitled "Bankruptcy," it would really not be a complete source guide without it.

Bankruptcy sort of sneaks up on entrepreneurs like a summer cold. And once you get it, it is hard to get rid of. Just like the common cold, there are really no cures—only aspirin to help relieve the symptoms. The sources of help here will familiarize you with the various issues in bankruptcy. Many small businesses find themselves or their customers or their suppliers in bankruptcy and are totally unable to cope with the problem. Unfortunately, many entrepreneurial ventures never come out of a Chapter 11 and die without a second birth. Roughly, half of the small companies in the country are unable to survive a Chapter 11. Yet, keep in mind that Henry Ford, the premier entrepreneur, who started the Ford Motor Company, failed twice before he succeeded. Bankruptcy is really not a bad thing, but it does hold bad connotations.

Kits of bankruptcy forms are available from:

American Bankruptcy
  Council
2525 Van Ness Avenue
San Francisco, CA 94109

Dephic Press
Belli Building
San Francisco, CA 94111

Bankruptcy: Problems, Process & Reform integrates bankruptcy with other economic and social events. It sets bankruptcy into proper perspective in the American scene. The Brookings Institute is a high-quality source of original information about economic issues and this book is an excellent reference. Write:

The Brookings Institute
1775 Massachusetts
   Avenue, N.W.
Washington, D.C. 20036

The Complete Guide to Getting Yourself Out of Debt is a practical manual for everyone who needs urgent relief from the tensions of debt. The author, president of Family Financial Planners, explains how to stop bill collectors, suits, garnishments, and wage attachments; how to wipe out old debts without borrowing or bankruptcy—and retain AAA credit; how to set up a workable family budget—and much more. It's especially helpful for an individual. Write:

Frederick Fell Publishers,
   Inc.
386 Park Avenue, South
New York, NY 10016
(212)685-9017

The Credit Executive is published by the New York Credit & Financial Management Association exclusively for its members; the subscription charge is included in the membership fee. Occasionally, special provisions are made for universities, government agencies, or even an interested individual. The publication features articles of interest to middle and top executives in commercial credit and finance. It also has articles legislation and court decisions having a bearing on these fields.

A number of handbooks are also available to the general public for $6.00 each. Current titles are listed as follows:

1. A Practical Guide to Chapter XI of the Bankruptcy Act.
2. What the Businessman Should know About Commercial Arbitration.
3. What the Business Executive Should Know About the Uniform Commercial Code.
4. Guarantees and Subordinations.

Write:

Credit Executive
71 West 23rd Street
New York, NY 10010
(212)741-4743

The Guide to Personal Bankruptcy is a workbook for bankruptcy. Complete with sample forms and copies of actual forms needed to be used for filing, it's a step-by-step workbook of the bankruptcy process. Its common language makes it worth reading. Write:

Crown Publishing
  Company
419 Park Avenue, South
New York, NY 10016

How to Get Out if You're in Over Your Head is a large workbook with practical advice on how to get out of debt. Write:

Enterprise Publishing
1000 Oakfield Dane Field
Wilmington, DE 19810

The National Bankruptcy Reporter is an interesting newsletter that exists to inform you of business bankruptcy filings above a certain size all across the country. It lists the vital data on each new filing. It's expensive, over $1,000 annually, but it provides useful data on a subject that can be hard to learn or acquire information about. Write:

National Bankruptcy
  Reporter
Andrews Publications,
  Inc.
1634 Latimer Street
Philadelphia, PA 19103

Strategies and Techniques for Saving the Financially Distressed Small Business, written by a practicing attorney, shows business people how to protect themselves from overzealous creditors and how to turn their business adversity around. It offers an overview of some of the remedies that are available. With this information, businesses that can survive will learn, in fact, how to survive. Write:

Pilot Books
347 Fifth Avenue
New York, NY 10016
(212)685-0736

Ten Cents on the Dollar is an extremely easy to read and understandable book on the ins and outs of bankruptcy. Its light touch is
valuable because it offers an insight into why 10 cents on the dollar
is a common slogan for bankruptcy. Write:

Ten Cents on the Dollar
Simon & Schuster
Rockefeller Center
630 Fifth Avenue
New York, NY 10020

FEDERAL REFORM OF BANKRUPTCY CODE

The Bankruptcy Reform Act of 1978 became effective October 1,
1979. This long-awaited revision of the bankruptcy code has many
advantages for creditors. It might be wise to review the code in total
and reexamine your firm's credit policies. Here are some highlights
of the new procedures.

1. Previously, Chapter 10 was used for larger, publicly held
companies and Chapter 11 was for small entrepreneurial ventures.
The reorganization effectively eliminates any distinction among
business entities. Hence, Chapter 11 can now be available to both
publicly owned companies, to partnerships, and to sole proprietor-
ships.

2. The bankruptcy court has greater power and can settle a
greater range of issues that previously had to be heard in other
courts. In addition, procedural delays have been removed, no longer
requiring cumbersome mechanics to become operational.

3. Either a creditor or a debtor can petition for the debtor's
reorganization whereas previously debtors were the only ones who
could petition for reorganization and creditors had to petition for
liquidation.

4. A creditor can reclaim goods from an unpaid invoice from an

insolvent buyer within 10 days of sale. This now corresponds with the Uniform Commercial Code (UCC).

We suggest that you send for a free copy of the Bankruptcy Reform Act T.L. 98-598 by writing:

House of Documents
    Room
8226 Capital Building
Washington, D.C. 20515

C. Barter Clubs

The barter clubs and publication listed below are geared primarily to the self-employed or small businesspersons and offer an alternative to increasing your cash outlay. For exchanges with subsidiary offices in several states, the address of the exchange's headquarters is listed. These offices can be contacted for more information about barter clubs in your area.

Atwood Richards, Inc.
99 Park Avenue
New York, NY 10016

Barter Billionaire
Lock Box 983, Dept. E-1
W. Caldwell, NJ 07006

Barter Communique
6500 Midnight Pas Road
Penthouse Suite 504
Sarasota, FL 33581
(813) 349-2242
This is a quarterly barter publication with a circulation of close to 50,000. The price is $10 annually.

Business Exchange, Inc.
4716 Vineland Avenue
North Hollywood, CA
    91602

Business Owners' Exchange
4901 W. 77th Street, Suite 123-B
Minneapolis, MN 55435

Exchange Enterprises
159 West Haven Avenue
Salt Lake City, UT 84115
Attention: Ross Rigby or
    Gaylen Rigby
(Branch offices in 14 western and mid-western states, Alaska, and Hawaii.

For more information about an office in your area, write to the exchange headquarters at the address above.)

Hilton Exchange
5034 Lankersheim
  Boulevard
North Hollywood, CA
  91601
Attention: M. Hilton

International Trade
  Exchange, Inc.
7656 Burford Drive
McLean, VA 22101
  Attention: Clyde
  Fabretti, Director of
  Marketing

The parent company has issued licenses to owner-operators in 40 cities throughout the country and is planning offices in several other cities in the near future. For further information about an exchange office in your area, write to the ITE headquarters at the address above.

Mutual Credit Buying
6420 Wilshire Boulevard
Los Angeles, CA 90048
Attention: Tom Skala,
  President

The Learning Exchange
Box 920
Evanston, IL 60204

Useful Services Exchange
% Wellborn Company
1614 Washington Plaza
Reston, VA 22090

D. Business Plans

A document written to articulate the directions of a growing business enterprise is a business plan. These road maps are often written to raise new money for an expanding business. Internal and external entrepreneurs write them to show the obvious strengths of their business. Below are discussed several sources to help in the preparation of these plans.

One of the finest pieces of information for understanding financial statements is offered free of charge by the world's largest securities firm, Merrill Lynch, Pierce Fenner & Smith. This 24-page book, entitled *Understanding Financial Statements* is so good it is often used as a free handout in graduate-level college finance courses. It offers an understanding of the three basic financial tools: Balance Sheet, Cash Flow Statement, and Profit and Loss Statement.

You can call your local Merrill Lynch office, which can be found in your local directory, and ask for a copy.

Several excellent articles on developing a business plan are contained within the books offered by the most professional source of venture capital information, Capital Publishing Company. Although these books are a bit expensive, some of the articles on the business plan are truly excellent because the tips are practical and worthwhile. Write:

Stan Pratt
Capital Publishing
2 Laurel Street
Wellesley Hills, MA
(617)235-5405

The Entrepreneur's Handbook is an excellent book of readings for entrepreneurs. This two-volume handbook is described as excellent because the books contain all the good articles on business plans (plus other entrepreneurial subjects) ever written. There are six articles on how to prepare a business plan in these two volumes. Write:

Artec House
610 Washington Street
Dedham, MA 02026
(617)326-8220

or
The Center for
   Entrepreneurial
   Management
311 Main Street
Worcester, MA 01608
(617)755-0770

The Small Business Administration offers several excellent pamphlets on writing a business plan. These are very inexpensive and surprisingly good. They even offer further information on where to obtain information on writing a business plan. Contact your local SBA field office for current information.

Small Marketeer Aid #153
Business Plan for Retailer (24 pages)
Small Marketeer Aid #150
Business Plan for Retailer (24 pages)
Management Aid for Small Manufacturers #218
Business plan for small manufacturers (22 pages)

A new center was established in February, 1978 to speed up the delivery process of SBA pamphlets. All requests to this high-speed center should be on SBA form 115A, which is a list of available SBA publications. Form 115A can be requested from the center. Write:

The Small Business
   Administration
Box 15434
Fort Worth, Texas 76119

The nationwide toll-free Watts number 800-433-7272. In Texas call 800-792-8901. The telephone recording service is available 24 hours per day, seven days per week.

Another source of information on a business plan's development is a two-part document. Part I is a five-page approach to developing a business plan, and Part II describes how to prepare a business plan. It costs $30.00.

Institute for New
   Enterprise
   Development
385 Concord Avenue
Belmont, MA 02178
(617)489-3950

E. Entreprenuerial Education

A small but fascinating school for entrepreneurs is housed in a quaint inn in the beautiful village of Londonderry, Vermont. It's headed by two men:

> Brian Smith head of the business department at Franklin Pierce College, founder of a New England-based electronic medical instruments company and a former IBMer.
>
> James S. Howard founder of the Country Business Brokers in Brattleboro, Vermont, and a former public relations executive on Madison Avenue.

The seminar program they offer is couple-oriented, with small classes appropriate to the charming setting. The fee is $260 per couple for a weekend. Couples are recruited primarily through newspaper advertisements, and the operations of the inn are often cited as an example of those of a small business of your own. For more information write to:

> The Country Business
>   Brokers
> 225 Main Street
> Brattleboro, VT 05301
> (802)254-4504

Tarrytown, New York, is a half hour north of Manhattan at the Tappan Zee bridge. This lovely town is the home of Robert L. Schwartz's charming 26-acre Tarrytown Conference Center. What makes it "the best" is owner/entrepreneur/counterculturist/humanist Bob Schwartz.

Schwartz runs a School for Entrepreneurs (which already has several hundred graduates) over two consecutive weekends several times a year. It's good, if not great. Besides all the knowledge they give you about how to start your own business, these seminars provide a special sense of community and sharing. It's a warm place where you have a chance to unwind and grow.

Below are some excerpts from school's brochure.

In a time of accelerating personal and social change, new-type entrepreneurs are needed to create more sensitive ideas, services, and products.

The creation of a business venture embodying personal vision is a powerful route to personal growth and fulfillment as well as profit.

The school uses a high-intensity, total-immersion, experimental method familiar to students of personal development courses by transferring these techniques to the hard-nosed marketplace. The School for Entrepreneurs is a leader in applying personal growth techniques to business judgment and career planning.

The School for Entrepreneurs trains Americans for what the Buddhists call Right Livelihood, the fullest use of one's total self in the pursuit of a noble concept.

Interested? Write:

Bob Schwartz
The School for
  Entrepreneurs
Tarrytown House
East Sunnyside Lane
Tarrytown, NY 10591
(212)WE3-1232
(914)LY1-8200

Another school of entrepreneurs is headed by William J. McCrea, the chairman of the Entrepreneurship Institute. This school moves from city to city and offers weekend training seminars entitled "How to Create and Manage Your Own Business." The fee is just under $300. For a schedule, call or write to:

The Entrepreneurship
  Institute
90 East Wilson Bridge
  Road
Suite 247
Worthington, OH 43085
(614)885-0585

Dr. Leon Danco of the University Services Institute in Cleveland, Ohio, offers a host of interesting family-oriented business seminars.

Dr. Danco is one of the finest authorities on the father–son team and on issues of families within small business.

University Services
  Institute
5862 Mayfield Road
Box 24197
Cleveland, Ohio 44124
(216)442-0800

A group of intense, get-away-from-it-all seminars is offered by Marshall Thurber, nestled in the woods of Vermont near the Canadian Border. The seminars are usually long and intense, but always very good. Write:

Marshall Thurber Burklyn
  Enterprise
1700 Montgomery
Suite 230
San Francisco, CA 94111

or

Marshall Thurber
East Burke
Vermont 05832
(802)626-9332

or

Marshall Thurber
1288 Rimer Drive
Morage, CA 94556
(415)376-2827

If you have ever felt that penetrating the U.S. government was like kicking a two-hundred-foot sponge, help is now available. The Small Business Administration (SBA) appointed an exceptionally qualified individual to its newly created post of Small Business Advocacy. This means that his tax-payer-funded job is to champion entrepreneurial causes. He will tell you where the SBA is offering seminars in your area. Do you need help of any kind or do you offer positive suggestions? Write:

Mr. Milton Stewart
Chief of Advocacy
Small Business
  Administration
1441 L Street, N.W.
Washington, D.C. 20416

The East-West Center is a resource systems institute that assists small business people in identifying and developing their entrepreneurial capabilities and in originating or finding new enterprise opportunities suited to local conditions. It is one of the international meeting places for entrepreneurs of varying cultures and backgrounds. Its report entitled *Entrepreneurial Discovery and Development* is an excellent source of help. Write:

The East-West Center
1777 East-West Road
Honolulu, HI 96848

HELP FROM COLLEGES FOR SMALL BUSINESSES

University Business Development Centers (UBDCs) are funded by government agencies (usually the Small Business Administration (SBA)) and are affiliated with local universities. They are charged with helping small businesses grow and prosper within a specific region. They can be of specific assistance, especially in the development of a business plan, and they are currently operational at the following colleges. As this listing goes to print, other colleges are launching SBDCs, so be sure to inquire in your area. This is an outgrowth of the SBA's Small Business Institute (SBI) program. Under the SBI program, local colleges and the SBA send 5,000 to 10,000 student teams to help small businesses annually. They can help and they are free, so it may pay to find out about the SBI college serving your area.

Also, in each of the 10 regions of the United States, as segmented by the SBA, a faculty member at a specific university is the regional coordinator of the SBI.

An excellent newsletter exists on the SBI program and provides continuing help for entrepreneurs:

Small Business Institute
Directors Asssociaton
Editor, Dr. Kenneth D.
  Douglas
University of Northern
  Colorado
School of Business
Greeley, CO 80639

The National Science Foundation (NSF) under the direction of Robert M. Colton has been the champion of this worthwhile cause. The NSF has sponsored three university-based innovation centers. While these centers have an engineering overtone, they do indeed assist the entrepreneur.

A copy of an evaluation report of the three existing innovation centers can be obtained from:

Research Triangle
  Institute
P.O. Box 12194
Research Triangle Park
North Carolina 27709
(919)541-6000

Below are the innovation centers currently operating:

Dr. Gerald G. Udell
University of Oregon
Eugene, OR 97403
(503)686-3111

Prof. Yaa Tzu Li
MIT, School of Engineering
77 Massachusetts Avenue
Cambridge, MA 02139
(617)253-1000

Prof. Dwight M. Bauman
Carnegie-Mellon University
Frew Avenue
Margaret Morrison
Pittsburg, PA 15213
(412)578-2000

SMALL BUSINESS DEVELOPMENT CENTER

Small Business Development Centers (SBDCs) are sources of management assistance for persons who are operating a small business or contemplating launching a new business. They are located on university campuses and are funded by the Small Business Administration. There are presently sixteen operational SBDCs located throughout the country.

California State
  Polytechnic University
Pomona, CA

California State
  University
Chico, CA

Rutgers University
New Brunswick, N.J.

University of Georgia
Athens, Georgia

University of Missouri
St. Louis, MO

University of Nebraska
Omaha, NE

University of Southern
  Maine
Portland, ME

University of West
  Florida
Pensacola, FL

Howard University
  District of Columbia

University of Wisconsin
Madison, WI

University of S. Carolina
Columbia, S. Carolina

Wharton School of
  Finance
University of
  Pennsylvania
Philadelphia, PA

St. Cloud University
St. Cloud, MN

University of Arkansas
Fayetteville, AK

University of Utah
Salt Lake City, Utah

Washington State
  University
Pullman, WA

ENTREPRENEUR'S EDUCATION

Karl Vesper of the University of Washington in Seattle has the enviable record of being three professors in one: mechanical engineering, business administration, and marine biology. However, he is best known for his work as scorekeeper of academic courses of small business and entrepreneurship. He recently surveyed 610 schools of business and 243 schools of engineering and based on a response of 61% and 48% respectively, here is what he found:

These are data for teaching new ventures, not the more popular small business management type of course. There are about 30 schools of engineering that teach entrepreneurship, according to Vesper. The remainder are business schools.

Total number of schools offering courses in new ventures

Year	1968	1970	1972	1974	1976	1978	Planned
	8	29	47	75	105	137	215

Vesper distributes a detailed list of schools and course descriptions that is available by writing to:

The Center for Venture
 Management
207 E. Buffalo Street
Milwaukee, WI 53202

Furthermore, as the scorekeeper, Vesper has begun keeping score of the emergence of academic chairs in dual fields of entrepreneurship and free enterprise. According to Vesper's early data, the endowed chairs are primarily in the field of private (free) enterprise, with a minority in the field of entrepreneurship.

COLLEGES AND UNIVERSITIES WITH ESTABLISHED ENTREPRENEURIAL AND FREE ENTERPRISE CHAIRS AND PROGRAMS

American International College
Applachian State University
Augusta College
Babson Institute
Baylor University
Birmingham-Southern College

Brescia College
Brunswick Junior College
George Peabody College
Georgia State University
Harding College
John Carroll University
Kent State University
Lamar University
Lambuth College
Loyola University of Chicago
North Georgia College
Northeast Louisiana University

Ohio State University
Purdue University
Samford University
Southwest Baptist College
Texas A&M University
Texas Christian University
University of Akron
University of Indiana
University of Oklahoma
University of Tennessee, Chattanooga
University of Texas, Austin
University of Wisconsin, Madison
Washington University
Wharton School
Wichita State University

Further information about endowed chairs like these is available from two sources. Richard Emerson and John L. Ward, School of Business, Loyola University, 820 North Michigan Avenue, Chicago, IL, 60601, have prepared a paper summarizing chairs in existence or being planned at 59 colleges and universities. Craig Aranoff is President of the Association for Chairs of Private Enterprise, centered at the School of Business, Georgia State University, Atlanta, GA 30303.

BABSON COLLEGE'S ENTREPRENEURIAL HALL OF FAME, WELLESLEY, MASSACHUSETTS

RECIPIENTS FOR 1978

Kenneth H. Olsen is the president of Digital Equipment Corporation, which was founded in 1957. It was a new idea to start a company at this time of recession when a number of new companies were in trouble. With only $70,000 to work with, every dollar was carefully watched and most of the work from cleaning the floors to making their own tools was done by Olsen and his associates. He started with the ideas of no government funding for their research, and they sought to make a profit from day one.

Berry Gordy, the president and chairman of Motown Industries, Inc., loved writing and creating songs. His first record store in Detroit was opened in 1953, and in 1955 he was bankrupt. After not being able to collect from a publisher who owed him $1,000, he decided to start a company for young writers. He was told that he could not do it. That was all he needed to hear, and Motown was born. He believes that you must first consider happiness before success so that success does not destroy you later.

Royal Little is the former chairman of Textron, Inc. He used his textile business to expand into more diversified areas of industry. He believed that if one business is not performing, get out—sell it, and then buy another one. His idea worked, and this started the conglomerate trend in the United States.

Ray Kroc, chairman of the McDonald Corporation, started out with the Lily Cup Company, and sold paper cups for about 17 years. As a salesman for a multiple milkshake mixer, the Multi-Mixer, he heard of an operation in California run by the McDonald brothers. Their stand was using eight of these mixers, making up to 40 milkshakes at one time. After his association with the McDonalds, Kroc felt that he was growing faster than they were, and in 1954 he opened his first "McDonalds." In 1960 he bought the business for $1.5 million. His theory is that "part of being an entrepreneur is knowing what to give and when to give it."

Soichiro Honda founded the Honda Motor Company 30 years ago. He first brought motorcycles to the United States 20 years ago, and thus created a new product. His first task was to sell the United States on motorcycling; then he had to sell Honda. He is not sure that he is an entrepreneur, only that he is a man with imagination, creativity, and desire behind him.

1979 Recipients

John Eric Jonsson, 77, is the founder and former chairman of Texas Instruments. After graduating from Renssalaer Polytechnic Institute in 1922, he became interested in Texas Instruments, then Geophysical Services, Inc., in Newark, NJ. The outfit moved to Texas in 1934, and Jonsson and Eugene McDermott bought out what is now a billion-dollar concern.

Diane Von Furstenburg, president of DVF, Inc., came to the United States in 1969 and saw a great need in the fashion industry. She designed a basic dress, in a basic material called jersey. Her claim to success is that you can be a woman and mother and be in business, too, if you are willing to work, plan, and discipline yourself.

John H. Johnson is the founder of *Ebony* magazine. Poverty motivated him to work harder in high school, which earned him a scholarship to the University of Chicago. In his junior year, he worked on a company magazine, which gave him the idea to publish a *Negro Digest* similar to the *Reader's Digest*. The profits he received from this magazine enabled him to start *Ebony* magazine.

Thomas Mello Evans is the chairman of Crane Company, which manufactures everything from steel to antipollution gear. He took over Crane Company in 1959, and more recently purchased 7.3% of the outstanding common stock of MacMilan, Inc. the broadly based purchaser. He has always shown a profit, and companies usually succeed under his management.

Byung Chull Lee, chairman of Samsung Group, started a rice cleaning plant in South Korea in 1935. After deciding that his country could prosper only through trade, he established the Samsung (Three-Start) export-import company in 1952. Today, as Korea's richest man, his fortune is over $500 million, and Samsung has become a 24-company conglomerate with sales of $2 billion per year.

1980 Recipients

1. Mary Wells Lawrence of Wells, Rich, Greene and Company.
2. L. Lehrman of the Rite-Aid and Lehrman Institute.
3. Mary Hudson of the Hudson Oil Company.
4. Peter Grace of W.R. Grace and Company

F. Exporting

If you feel that your firm's production capacity warrants looking into foreign markets for your products, the U.S. Commerce Department has three excellent programs to offer.

SALES REPRESENTATIVES

To find an agent or distributor, you must complete an application form that includes a brief description of the products for sale and the qualifications required by an agent or distributor (type of customers served, products handled, etc.). This information is relayed to the relevant U.S. Foreign Service post, which attempts to identify up to six agents or distributors (in the country or countries you have specified), who are interested in your proposal. In about 60 days, you will receive the names and addresses of potential sales agents to contact and a description of their operations. The fee for this service is $25.00 per country.

SALES INQUIRIES

The Trade Opportunities Program (TOP) helps in developing sales leads for United States suppliers. The one-time fee is $37.50 to have your business's individual registered code entered into the TOP computer in Washington. This code includes the products you sell, the countries in which you want them to be sold, and whether you want to deal directly with a buyer or through an agent or distributor. The inquiries are originated by the employees in 200 American embassies and consulates located in over 120 foreign countries who continually send data on foreign buyers' needs to Washington, D.C. You will receive a listing of the inquirers' names and addresses when one of the foreign sales inquiries matches your code.

MAILING LISTS

The Export Contact List Service will help you compile a mailing list. This is a computerized version of the Commerce Department's old "trade lists." It includes information on over 140,000 manufacturers, service organizations, agents, distributors, retailers, and cooperatives in 143 countries. The cost of a list is $10.00 for set-up and 6 cents per name. One or two duplicate mailing lists may be obtained at $3.00 each. For an additional charge, the names can be printed on gummed mailing labels. Look in your telephone book for the Commerce Department nearest you or write to the U.S. Department of Commerce, Washington, D.C.

OTHER SOURCES OF HELP

"Market Match" in New York conducts a trade lead service similar to the Commerce Department's TOP. This program is also an on-line computerized directory of buyers and sellers worldwide. Write to:

Gerald Lieberman
World Trade Center
New York, NY 10048
(212)466-3067

If you have a question concerning selling your products abroad, you can call Export-Import Bank on its new toll-free hot line (800)424-5201, which was set up to help small business exporters contact an expert in the field to develop questions on doing business overseas.

EXPORT LOANS FROM SBA

The Small Business Administration (SBA) has $100 million available for loan guarantees for small business exporters. If your firm cannot secure bank debt on its own and would like to begin or expand into foreign markets, it is eligible for these loans. The money is actually distributed by the bank or financial institution, and the SBA offers its usual percentage type of guarantee. The use of the funds is extremely discretionary, including trips abroad or visiting trade shows. Application for this type of loan should be made through a local bank. Furthermore, the SBA has a new export program for the Procurement Automated Source System. It's known as PASS, and its purpose is to inform United States suppliers of export programs and seminars. You can register at your local SBA office with the Procurement Assistance Division for this PASS program.

Howard V. Perlmutter, professor at the University of Pennsylvania's Wharton School, an expert on multinational organizations, says that " . . . a wild game is about to begin. It's called how many of our companies can make it in world markets and how do we get them there?" (*Business Week*, July 2, 1979)

If you, as a venturesome entrepreneur are considering the foreign market, the following sources of information can be used to explore most areas of such an undertaking. Write:

Director, Bureau of
    Export Development
U.S. Department of
    Commerce
Washington, D.C. 20230

Programs to write for from the Dept. of Commerce include the following:

Foreign Trader's Index
Trade Opportunities
    Program (TOP)
Export Contact List
    Service
World Traders Report
Commerce Business Daily

Export-Import Bank of
    the U.S.
811 Vermont Avenue,
    N.W.
Washington, D.C. 20571

Director
Export Trade Services
  Division
Foreign Agricultural
  Service
U.S. Dept. of Agriculture
Washington, D.C. 20250
(202)447-6343

Federal Trade
  Commission
Public Reference Branch
6th Street & Pennsylvania
  Ave.
Room 130
Washington, D.C. 20580
(202)523-3830

Department of the
  Treasury
U.S. Customs Service
1303 Constitution Ave.
  N.W.
Washington, D.C. 20520
(202)566-8195

Office of Commercial
  Affairs
Bureau of Economic and
  Business Affairs
Room 33-34
U.S. State Department
Washington, D.C. 20520
(202)632-8097

Market Match
Gerald Lieberman
World Trade Center
New York, NY 20048
(212)466-3067

PUBLICATIONS

Government and Business: A Joint Venture in International Trade (free booklet published by the U.S. State Department's Office of Commercial Affairs). To order, write to:

Office of Public Affairs
U.S. State Department
Room 48-27A
Washington, D.C. 20520
(202)632-6575

Guide to United Nations Conference of Trade and Development (UNCTAD) Publications (free catalog published by UNCTAD). Write:

United Nations Sales
Section
Editorial & Document
Section
Palais Des Nations 1211
Geneva 10, Switzerland

Lorna M. Daniells,
*Business Information
Sources*, (Berkeley, CA;
University of California
Press, 1976) publishes a
list of reference data
sources for exporters.

*Quarterly Economic
Review* (London,
England: Economist
Intelligence Unit),
reviews 45 countries
quarterly.

OECD Economic Surveys
(Paris, France:
Organization for
Economic Cooperation
and Development),
individual, annual
reviews listed by
country.

*Investing, Licensing and
Trading Conditions
Abroad,* (New York,
NY: Business
International), two
volumes.

The Department of Commerce provides free consultation with an expert trade specialist who can help answer questions about the feasibility of exporting your product to other countries, government regulations, cultural mores, and competition. Bankers in the international departments of major city banks are also good contacts to help assess a foreign market. A third source of information about export possibilities is foreign students at your local universities who can suggest marketing potential and possible cultural and governmental limitations.

G. Grants

In 1977 over 26,000 United States foundations gave away close to $3 billion in grants. The federal government, mostly the Department of Health, Education and Welfare, gave away over $60 billion. Very few of these grants were awarded to small businesses. Although it is true that 95% of the grant proposals submitted are rejected, it is also true that small businesses seldom seek or receive financial grants.

A special exemption is needed to give a grant to profit-seeking business, but it is not uncommon for a grant to be awarded for a project to a nonprofit organization (such as a college or university) and that an entrepreneur will be a subcontractor on the project. It may be very much in your interest, therefore, to support the efforts of local nonprofit institutions to obtain funds. Information on oraganizations that give grants can be obtained by consulting the following sources.

1. The Foundation Center, an information clearing house that maintains national libraries in Chicago, New York City, and Washington, D.C. as well as regional libraries in 48 states, Mexico, and Puerto Rico. These libraries are open to the public at no charge.

2. The *Foundation Directory*, a reference work which lists 2,800 foundations that awarded $1.8 billion in grants in 1976. The directory gives the following data on the foundations it lists: names and addresses (by state); founders' names; total assets; officials' names; purposes and activities; and the number and dollar amount of grants awarded during the year. This directory is available at any large library.

3. The *Foundation Grants Index*, which lists grants of more than $5,000 made by the 300 major foundations. It lists the names of the recipients, the purposes of the grants, and the dollar amounts awarded. A separate "Key Word & Phrase" index is especially useful in determining the current real interests of each foundation. This book is also available in most large libraries.

4. The *Catalog of Federal Domestic Assistance and the Annual Register of Grant Support*. This is the single best starting point for research on grants. For information on obtaining a copy write:

Marquis Who's Who
4300 West 62nd Street
Indianapolis, IN 46206

The Register lists procedures for requesting grants; programs; names of agency officers; and the total number of applications received and awarded by programs each year.

Information about Premium and Incentive Buying

Many products can be sold to companies or organizations that will use them as premiums or giveaways, or in incentive buying programs. Perhaps your product(s) can be used in this way. For a list of such buyers, there are several sources you can contact:

The Salesmen's Guide
1182 Broadway
New York, NY 10001

Incentive Marketing
633 Third Avenue
New York, NY 10017
(212)986-4800
Circulation: about 35,000

Premium/Incentive
   Business
1515 Broadway
New York, NY 10036
(212)869-1300
Circulation: about 24,000

NPSE Newsletter
1600 Route 22
Union, NY 07083
(201)687-3832
Circulation: about 2,000

FREE PUBLICITY

Rather than launching a marketing program with a series of paid-for advertisements, consider the advantages of a publicity release program. Your firm may be eligible for news releases or product releases or literature releases, all of which are free. Doesn't it make sense to have all initial effort directed toward the free material? Entrepreneurial managers obtain all the available free product releases before they succumb to paid-for advertisements.

The procedure for contacting the various trade journals varies from industry to industry. Some journals require black-and-white photographs, others require color photographs, and others accept no photographs. To obtain specific information on how to obtain publicity and to obtain a list of relevant trade journals, these four publishers offer you directories and publicity release programs.

Ayer's Directory of
  Newspapers and
  Periodicals
William J. Luedke,
  Publisher; Ayer Press
210 West Washington
  Square
Philadelphia, PA 19106
(215)829-4472

Ayer's Directory is the most comprehensive source of newspaper information.

Bacon's Publicity Checker
14 East Jackson Boulevard
Chicago, IL 60604

For an excellent overall list of periodicals, use the *Standard Periodical Directory* published by:

Oxbridge Publishing
  Company
383 Madison Avenue,
  Room 1108
New York, NY 10016
(212)189-8524

Ulrich's Directory of Periodicals is usually available in public libraries and as a reference in college libraries. It is published by:

R. Bowker Company
1180 Avenue of the
   Americas
New York, NY 10036
(212)764-5100

CLIPPING SERVICES

Below is a partial list of services that will clip newspaper and magazine articles about your company or about a product area. This can be a valuable service to keep you posted on the advertising and public relations efforts of your competitors as well as your own company's programs. *Note:* This list is only a partial list because no organization keeps this information on a national basis. We suggest that you inspect your local Yellow Pages to determine if such an organization exists in your geographical areas.

Allen's Press Clipping
   Bureau
657 Mission Street
San Francisco, CA 94105

Bacon's Clipping Service
14 East Jackson Boulevard
Chicago, IL 60604
(312)922-8419

Florida Clipping Service
Box 10278
Tampa, FL 33679
(813)831-0962

Luce Press Clipping
   Service
912 Kansas Avenue
Topeka, KS 66612
(913)232-0201

New England Newsclip
   Service
5 Auburn Street
Framingham, MA 01701
(617)879-4460

MARKETING SOURCES

The National Research Bureau is a subsidiary of the Automated Marketing Systems, Inc. It offers the *Gebbie House Magazine Directory*, which lists company house organs, newsletters, and internal company information. It is an often overlooked source of publicity.

This directory is a part of the *Working Press of Nations,* a five-volume set of invaluable aids to over 100,000 prime media contacts available from:

>   National Research Bureau
>   Headquarters
>   104 South Michigan
>   Avenue
>   Chicago, IL 60603
>   (312)641-2655

>   Editorial and Production
>   424 North Third Street
>   Burlington, IA 42601
>   (319)752-5415

>   Washington Bureau
>   1141 National Press
>   Building
>   Washington, D.C. 20045
>   (202)638-4746

Conventions and trade show listings are compiled and offered by:

>   Exhibits Schedule
>   144 East 44th Street
>   New York, NY 10017

>   The Hendrickson
>   Publishing Company
>   91 North Franklin Street
>   Hempstead, NY 11550
>   (516)483-6883

>   International Association
>   of Fairs and Exhibits
>   77 Arbor Road
>   Winston-Salem, NC
>   27104

>   Sales Meeting Magazines
>   144 East 44th Street
>   New York, NY 10017

Trade Show Week
1605
Cahuenga Boulevard
Los Angeles, CA 90028
(213)463-4891

I. Manufacturer's Representatives

How to select the proper manufacturer's representative for your product line is one of the most difficult questions facing an entrepreneurial venture. The following sources list several organizations and directories that will help find competent sales representatives for small businesses.

Albee-Campbell
806 Penn Avenue
Sinking Springs, PA
   19608
(215)678-3361

Representative Resources,
   Inc.
Drower Avenue
Thorndale, PA 19372
(215)383-1177

L. H. Simmonds, Inc.
60 East 42nd Street
New York, NY 10017
(212)889-1530

United Association of
   Manufacturers Agents
808 Broadway
Kansas City, MO 64105
(816)842-8130

Anthony J. Zinno
   Associates
2 Park Avenue
Manhasset, NY 10030
(516)627-2642

A group nearly 100 firms engaged in selling products and services to consumers, primarily in their homes, lists several directories of members that are available to member firms.

Direct Selling Association
1730 M Street N.W.
Suite 610
Washington, D.C. 20036
(202)293-5760

The Manufacturers Agents National Association is a 30-year-old industry association of manufacturers' agents and an excellent source of information. Write:

Manufacturers Agents
    National Association
2021 Business Center
    Drive
Box 16878
Irvine, CA 92713

The New England Manufacturing Exchange (NEMEX) is a clearinghouse that maintains up-to-date computerized information on products offered by some 1,400 suppliers. Both buyers and suppliers can obtain information on this nationwide free service by writing:

NEMEX
10 Moulton Street
Cambridge, MA 02138
(617)354-1150

Pacific International (President Gordon Strickler) takes the guesswork out of appointing reps. They have in their files a list of reps and rep companies in 42 major marketing areas in the United States and all foreign countries.

Pacific International
P.O. Box 894
Escondido, CA 92025
(714)745-7361

A directory listing more than 2,000 U.S. electronic representative firms and branches, indexed by geographical region and cross-indexed alphabetically, can be obtained from:

Electronic
    Representatives
    Association
233 East Erie Street
Chicago, IL 60611

They also offer a service including a listing in the ERA *Lines Available Bulletin*, issued monthly to some 1,500 members, designed to help manufacturers establish representation. In addition, they maintain a hotline service that enables manufacturers looking for reps in one or two markets to get their messages, within 36 hours, to representatives serving the defined territories.

Your ad in the *Manufacturers' Agents' Newsletter* reaches manufacturers throughout the United States and Canada and in some foreign countries whose principal method of selling their products is through manufacturer's representatives. Your ad in the newsletter can let these manufacturers know who you are, where you are, which territory you cover, and which product lines you are looking for.

Manufacturers' Agents'
    Newsletter, Inc.
23573 Prospect Avenue
Farmington, MI 58024

The Rep Information Service offers a wide range of assistance in securing manufacturer's representatives. The three fundamental publications offered are listed below. Write:

Rep Information Service
5521 Reseda Boulevard,
    Suite 17
Tarzana, CA 91356

Agent Edition, a
    published lead service
    giving sales agents in
    excess of 1,000 "Agents
    Wanted" leads during
    life of subscription,
    plus personal
    assistance in locating
    new product lines.

Agent Edition—Rep
    Information Service
5521 Reseda Boulevard,
    Suite 17
P.O. Box L
Tarzana, CA 91356
(213)705-1222

Manufacturers Edition is a lead service to help manufacturers find agents, manufacturers' representatives, and trading companies on a worldwide basis, plus regular mailings of published "Lines Wanted" listings, plus personal referral services to assist them in locating agents in specific territories.

Manufacturers' Edition—Rep Service (same as above) is a directory listing 1,235 moneymaking opportunity advertisements, complete with explanation of what was received in experience of answering all these offers, plus detailed explanation of illegal offers, postal regulations, schemes, chain letters, and how moneymaking opportunity offers work.

> Directory of 1,235
>   Opportunity Offers
> J.E. Distributing, Inc.,
>   Publisher
> 5521 Reseda Boulevard,
>   Suite 17
> Tarzana, CA 91356
> (213)705-1222

Rep World is a quarterly publication to about 5,000 which focuses on manufacturers' representatives.

> Rep World
> 578 Penn Ave.
> Sinking Spring, PA 19608

Specialty Salesmen and Business Opportunities is a monthly magazine on direct mailing and direct-to-consumer selling. A directory of agents is also available.

> *Specialty Salesmen and*
>   *Business Opportunities*
> 307 North Michigan
>   Avenue
> Chicago, IL 60601
> (312)726-0743

For a free ad in a weekly bulletin that goes to rep members in all fields, worldwide, write:

United Association
  Manufacturers' Reps
808 Broadway
Kansas City, MO 64105
(816)842-8130

Verified Directory of Manufacturers' Representatives is published biennially by Manufacturers' Agent Publishing Company. It presents a geographic listing of about 15,000 manufacturers' representatives (domestic and export) serving all industries, except food products, for the United States and Canada. It gives principal lines carried and trading areas covered.

A second publication lists more than 11,500 manufacturers who distribute through agents. Classified by industry, it includes name, address of manufacturer and principal products, credit ratings, and name and title of sales executives.

Manufacturers' Agents'
  Guide, $27.50.
National Association
  Diversified
  Manufacturers'
  Representatives
Manufacturers' Agents'
  Publishing Company,
  Inc.
663 Fifth Avenue
New York, NY 10022
(212)682-0326

Who's Who in Electronics lists 7,500 electronic manufacturers, 2,500 industrial electronic parts and equipment distributors, 3,300 independent electronic representative firms, together with a separate product index section with 1,600 product breakdowns, their manufacturers and distributors, It has information about products, sales, volume, marketing areas, key personnel, research facilities, telephone numbers, plant sizes, and new firms and information concerned with the electronics field.

B. Klein Publications
Box 8503

Coral Springs, FL 33065
(305)752-1708

The National Directory of Manufacturers' Representatives is a directory that will help you find reps on your own. The alphabetical listing of reps includes size of staff, geographic territories, products represented, markets served, and special services. A second section, listed by state, indicates the Standard Industrial Classification (SIC) codes for all the industries called on by reps in that state. Write:

McGraw-Hill Publishing
  Company
1221 Avenue of the
  Americas
New York, NY 10020

J. Patents, Inventions, Trademarks and Laboratories

How to Get a Patent is about America's patent law. For a copy of the booklet, write:

Consumer Information
  Center
Department 126E
Pueblo, CO 81009

The Inventors News, published by the Inventors Club of America, offers information on protection before patent, marketing and manufacturing, and development. The Inventors Club of America is a non-profit organization established to help inventors who are willing to help themselves. They show you ways to develop and market your ideas yourself. Write:

Inventors News
Box 3799

Springfield, MA 01101
(413)737-0670

or

Inventors Club of
    America
National Headquarters
1562 Main Street
Box 3799
Springfield, MA 01001
(413)737-0670

Action is published regularly to serve as a medium of commun-
ciation between members of the Association for the Advancement
of Invention and Innovation. It is open to inventors, entrepreneurs,
research directors, business people, scientists, engineers, lawyers,
patent attorneys and agents, educators, patent examiners, econo-
mists, and others who support the objectives of the Association.
Write:

The Association for the
    Advancement of
    Invention and
    Innovation
Suite 301, Crystal Mall 1
1911 Jefferson David
    Highway
Arlington, VA 22202

New Products and Processes Newsletter, a publication of *Newsweek
Magazine,* Inc., is a source for the most comprehensive, timely, and
usable new product information available anywhere. Each issue
contains reviews of 75 to 100 new products and processes, including
complete product descriptions, many with illustrations, availability
for manufacturing, and sales of licensing arrangements. Write:

New Products and
    Processes
Newsweek International
444 Madison Avenue
New York, NY 10022

New Tech is a new publication for an entrepreneur, or a small business person/investor. It will help you to keep up to date on new technology as it relates to entrepreneurial opportunity. Write:

New Tech
1212 Avenue of the
  Americas
New York, NY 10036

The United States Trademark Association is a nonprofit organization dedicated to the protection, development, and promotion of the trademark concept. USTA is the only organization in the United States totally devoted to trademarks, protecting the rights of trademark owners as well as communicating with business educators, the press, and the public to foster understanding and appreciation of the role of trademarks. The services offered by USTA concern all aspects of the trademark field: federal, state, and foreign legislation; education, promotion advertising, and merchandising; publicity and use by the press; proper handling of trademarks by corporate personnel, sales staff, dealers; and more. An important caveat: The services of USTA do not purport to substitute for or duplicate in any way the advice of legal counsel. To obtain information about ordering any of their publications, write:

The United States
  Trademark Association
6 East 45th Street
New York, NY 10017

WHERE TO GET HELP ON PATENTS AND LICENSING

Have a good idea? Is it patentable? Where can you turn for help? Here is a comprehensive listing of help available.

Inventors' associations. Arrange meetings with inventors to educate them in aspects of the patening process and the seeking of licenses:

Institute of American
  Inventors

635 F Street, NW
Washington, DC 20004
(202)737-6616

Inventors Assistance
  League, Inc.
1815 W. 6th Street
Los Angeles, CA 90057
(213)483-4850

Mortic Corp.
2030 E. 4th Street
Suite 149
Santa Ana, CA 92705
(714)835-4353

The United Inventors and
  Scientists of America
2503 W. 7th Street
Los Angeles, CA 90057
(213)389-3003

Alexander T. Marinaccio
Inventors Club of
  America
1562 Main Street
Box 3799
Springfield, MA 01101
(413)737-0670

Invention brokers. Firms specializing in getting licensor and licensee together:

Battelle Development
  Corp.
505 King Avenue
Columbus, OH 43201
(614)424-6424

Control Data Technotec,
  Inc.
8100 34th Avenue South
Minneapolis, Minn.

Dr. Dvorkovitz and
   Associates
P.Q. Box 1748
Ormond Beach, FL 32044
(904)677-7033

Eurosearch Marketing,
   Inc.
663 Fifth Avenue
New York, NY 10022
(212)355-5633

International Inventors,
   Inc.
Suite 309
4900 Leeburg Pike
Alexandria, VA 22303
(703)931-3130

Invention Marketing, Inc.
701 Smithville Street
12th Floor, Arott Building
Pittsburgh, PA 15222
(412)288-1300

Invention Marketing, Inc.
Suite L-5 The Vendome
160 Commonwealth
   Avenue
Boston, MA 02116
(617)266-7696

Kessler Sales Corp.
Kessler Bldg.
1247 Napoleon Street
Fremont, OH 43420
(419)332-6496

Licensing Management
   Corp.
80 Park Avenue
New York, NY 10016
(212)682-5944

Arthur D. Little, Inc.
Invention Management
   Corp.
Acorn Park
Cambridge, MA 02140
(617)864-5770

L and M Product Finders
752 Guinda
Palo Alto, CA 94301
(415)322-7082

Promotional Marketing,
   Inc.
615 Milwaukee Avenue
Glenview, IL 60025
(312)729-610

REFAC Technology
   Development Corp.
122 E. 42nd Street
New York, NY 10017
(212)687-4741

Research Corporation
405 Lexington Avenue
New York, NY 10016
(212)695-9301

University Patents, Inc.
2777 Summer Street
Stamford, CT 08905
(203)325-2285

Publications. Several specialized publications seek to match products offered for license with licensors:

American Bulletin of
   International
   Technology Transfer
International
   Advancement
5455 Wilshire Blvd.
Suite 1009
Los Angeles, CA 90036
(213)931-7481

International New
   Product Newsletter
Box 191
390 Stuart Street
Boston, MA 02117
(617)631-3225

New Products and
   Processes
Newsweek International
444 Madison Avenue
New York, NY 10022
(212)350-2000

Technology Mart
Thomas Publishing Co.
One Penn Plaza
New York, NY 10001
(212)695-0500

Technology Transfer
   Times
Benwill Publishers
167 Corey Road
Brookline, MA 02146
(617)212-5470

Institute for Inventions
   and Innovations, Inc.
85 Irving Street
Box 436
Arlington, MA 02174
(617)646-0093

One publisher produces two excellent newsletters on patents and inventions that may prove of interest to you:

1. *Invention Management.* An informational and educational journal for individuals and companies concerned with intellectual property. This is published monthly and costs $60.00 annually. It is excellent in the area of patents, technology transfer, and inventions.
2. *Copyright Management.* This is also published monthly and costs $60.00 annually. It deals with copyrights, licensing, and trademarks.

If you are interested in either monthly newsletter, write:

Richard A. Onanian
Institute for Invention &

Innovation, Inc.
85 Irving Street
Arlington, MA 02174
(617)646-0093

The Federal Laboratory Consortium (FLC) consists of the 180
federal research and development laboratories. In each there is a
person with the title "technical transfer representative," whose job
is to respond to questions from businesses. The good news is that
there is no charge. A directory is available from:

FLC Headquarters
Federal Laboratory
  Program Manager
National Science
  Foundation ISPT
Washington, D.C. 20050
(202)634-7996

A more expensive source of information exists at seven university-based technical information centers. An industrial application
study costs between $5,000 and $10,000, but literature searches are
also available. These centers draw on a vast array of business,
government, and trade organizations data. The locations are:

New England Research
  Applications Center
Mansfield Professional
  Park
Storrs, CT 06268

North Carolina Science
  and Technology
  Research Center
P.O. Box 12235
Research Triangle Park,
  NC 27709

Knowledge Availability
  Systems Center
University of Pittsburgh
Pittsburgh, PA 15260

Aerospace Research
  Application Center
Administration Building
1201 E. 38th Street
Indianapolis, IN 47401

Technology Use Studies
  Center
Southeastern Oklahoma
  State University
Durant, OK 74701

Technology Application
  Center
University of New
  Mexico,
Albuquerque, NM 87131

Western Research
  Application Center
University of Southern
  California
University Park
Los Angeles, CA 90007

K. Resource Organizations Serving Small Business

National Federation of
  Independent Business
490 L'Enfant Plaza East,
  S.W.
Washington, D.C. 20006

National Small Business
  Association
1604 K Street, N.W.
Washington, D.C. 20006

Center for Small Business
Chamber of Commerce of
  U.S.
1615 H Street, N.W.
Washington, D.C. 20062

COSIBA MEMBERS

Council of Smaller
  Enterprises
Mike Benz
690 Union Commerce
  Bldg.
Cleveland, OH 44115
(216)621-3300

Independent Business
   Association of
   Wisconsin
Jack Gardner
7635 Bluemound Rd.
Milwaukee, WI 53213
(414)258-7055

National Association of
   Small Business
   Investment Companies
Walter Stults
618 Washington Bldg.
Washington, D.C. 20005
(202)638-3411

National Business League
Sylvester Bass
4324 Georgia Avenue,
   N.W.
Washington, D.C. 20011
(202)726-7600

National Federation of
   Independent
   Businesses
James d. "Mike"
   McKevitt
490 L'Enfant Plaza East,
   S.W.
Washington, D.C. 20006

National Small Business
   Association
John Lewis
1604 K Street, N.W.
Washington, D.C. 20006

Small Business Council
Sandy Chadwick
One MONY Plaza, Suite
   1500
Syracuse, NY 13202

Smaller Business
   Association of New
   England
Lewis Shattuck
69 Hickory Drive
Waltham, MA 02154
(617)890-9070

Smaller Manufacturers
   Council
Leo McDonough
339 Boulevard of Allies
Pittsburgh, PA 15222
(412)391-1622

Small Business
   Legislative Council
Herbert Liebonson
1604 K Street, N.W.
Washington, D.C. 20006
(202)296-7400

SELECT STAFF, SBA OFFICE OF ADVOCACY

Office of Advocacy
Small Business
   Administration
1441 L Street, N.W.
Room 1010
Washington, D.C. 20416

Milton D. Stewart
Chief Counsel for
   Advocacy
(202)653-6984

David K. Voight
Executive Assistant
(202)653-6984

Thomas A. Gray
Administrative Officer
(202)653-6808

Jere Glover, Director
Office of Interagency
 Policy
(202)653-6213

David Metzger, Director
Office of Small Business
 Services Management
(202)653-6579

Fred A. Tarpley, Director
Office of Economic
 Research
(202)634-5886

Sally Bender, Director
Office of Women in
 Business
(202)634-6087

Robert E. Berney
Chief Economist
(202)634-4886

Christopher Burke
Advocate for Energy &
 Natural Resources
(202)653-6986

Victor M. Rivera
Advocate for Government
 Industry Relations
(202)653-6840

John S. Satagaj
Assistant Chief Counsel
 for State & Local
 Affairs
(202)653-6808

Susan M. Walthall
Field Activities
 Coordinator
(202)653-6808

Janice Somers
Trade Association
 Coordinator
(202)653-6808

STAFF OF THE HOUSE SMALL BUSINESS COMMITTEE

A reference list of people and committees in government who play major roles in the everyday operation of a smaller enterprise follows.

Thomas G. Powers
General Counsel
2361 Rayburn House
 Office Bldg.
(202)225-5821

Carol Clawson
Communications
 Specialist
2361 Rayburn House
 Office Bldg.
(202)225-6020

Raymond S. Wittig
Minority Counsel
B-343 Rayburn House
  Office Bldg.
(202)225-4038

Subcommittee on SBA
  and SBIC Authority
  and General Small
  Business Problems

Thomas G. Powers,
  General Counsel (see
  above)

Jordan Clark
Minority Subcommittee
  Counsel
2361 Rayburn House
  Office Bldg.
(202)225-4038

Subcommittee on General
  Oversight and Minority
  Enterprise

George Neidich
Subcommittee Counsel
2361 Rayburn House
  Office Bldg.
(202)225-4601

Subcommittee on
  Antitrust and Restraint
  of Trade Activities
  Affecting Small
  Business

Mark Rosenberg
Subcommittee
  Professional Staff
  Member
B-363 Rayburn House
  Office Bldg.
(202)225-8944

Karen Davis Hoppe
Minority Subcommittee
  Professional Staff
  Member
B-363 Rayburn House
  Office Bldg.
(202)225-4541

Subcommitee on Energy,
  Environment, Safety
  and Research

Mark Rosen
Subcommittee Counsel
B-363 Rayburn House
  Office Bldg.
(202)225-6026

Gregory S. Dole
Minority Subcommittee
  Counsel
B-363 Rayburn House
  Office Bldg.
(202)225-4541

Subcommittee on Access
  to Equity Capital and
  Business Opportunities

David E. Franasiak
Subcommittee Counsel
B-363 Rayburn Building
(202)225-7797

Harold L. Aronson
Minority Subcommittee
  Counsel
B-363 Rayburn House
  Office Bldg.
(202)335-4541

Subcommittee on Special
  Small Business
  Problems

Stephen P. Lynch
Subcommitee
  Professional Staff
  Member
B-363 Rayburn House
  Office Bldg.
(202)225-9368

WASHINGTON INFORMATION SOURCES

The Division of Information Services, Bureau of Labor Statistics has data available on employment, living conditions, prices, productivity, and occupational safety and health.

441 G Street, N.W.
Washington, D.C. 20212
(202)523-1239

The Bill Status Office will provide you with current status of any legislation or tell you if legislation has been introduced on a topic.

3669 HOBA#2
The LEGIS Office
Washington, D.C. 20515
(202)225-1772

The National Referral Center will find an organization willing to provide free information on any topic, for free.

Library of Congress
10 First Street, S.E.
Washington, D.C. 20540
(202)426-5670

The Federal Information Center will locate an expert in the federal government to tell you how the federal government can help you.

General Services
  Administration
7th and D. Streets, S.W.
Washington, D.C. 20407
(202)755-8660

Reference Section, Science and Technology Division offers both free and fee reference and bibliographic services.

> Library of Congress
> 10 First Street, S.E.
> Washington, DC 20540
> (202)426-5639

Data Users Services Division will identify census data on your topic.

> Bureau of the Census
> U.S. Department of
>   Commerce
> Washington, DC 20233
> (301)763-7662

Economics, Statistics, and Cooperative Service can provide the latest production and stock estimates for agricultural products as well as the supply-demand-price relationships and other economic factors.

> U.S. Department of
>   Agriculture
> Information Staff
> Washington, DC 20250
> (202)447-4230

Bureau of Domestic Business Development 100 industry analysts can provide or guide you to information on a company or industry.

> U.S. Department of
>   Commerce
> Washington, DC 20230
> (202)377-2786

Information Central will identify an association that can help with your problem, if you cannot find help in Gale's "Encyclopedia of Associations."

> American Society of
>   Association Executives
> 1101 16th Street, N.W.
> Washington, DC 20036
> (202)659-3333

Energy information sources are:

National Energy
  Information Center
Energy Information
  Administration
1726 M Street, N.W.
Washington, DC 20461
(202)566-9820

National Solar Heating
  and Cooling
  Information Center
P.O. Box 1607
Rockville, MD 20850
(800)523-2929

Technical Information
  Center
U.S. Department of
  Energy
Oak Ridge, TN 37830
(615)483-8611, ext. 34271

U.S. Civil Service Commission, Bureau of Manpower Information Systems has this material available: Civil Service employment, payroll information, and paydays (particularly useful in scheduling campaigns for consumer goods in Washington).

Manpower Statistics
  Division
1900 E Street, N.W.
Washington, DC 20415
(202)655-4000

U.S. Department of Commerce Census Bureau has this material available: General Census statistics, Census of Business, educational demographics, statistics on construction and other businesses in Washington area

Social and Economic
  Statistics
  Administration
Washington, DC 20233
(202)655-4000

U.S. Department of Labor has this material available: Cost of Living Index, monthly reports on employment by state and metro area, and general labor statistics.

> Bureau of Labor Statistics
> 441 G Street, N.W.
> Washington, DC 20210
> (202)393-2420

District of Columbia Government has this material available:General employment information and occupational make-up of the District of Columbia.

> Department of Manpower
> Community Relations
>   and Information
>   Division
> 500 C Street, N.W.
> Washington, DC 20011
> (202)393-6151

Metropolitan Washington Council of Governments has this material available: General statistical data and planned development information for the metropolitan Washington area.

> Information Services
> 1225 Connecticut Avenue,
>   N.W.
> Washington, DC 20036
> (202)223-6800

Washington Center for Metropolitan Studies has this material available: Population demographics and updated 1970 Census information.

> 1717 Massachusetts
>   Avenue, N.W.
> Washington, DC 20036
> (202)462-4868

USEFUL GOVERNMENT DATA

Materials that can be very beneficial to you are published by all the Nader groups. A wide variety of reports and publications is available. To obtain copies of the following free citizen action materials, send a self-addressed, stamped envelope to P.O. Box 19404, Washington, DC, 20036 (unless another address is indicated).

Public Citizen, Reports and Publications. A complete list of all reports and publications by Ralph Nader and other well-known consumer advocates.

Public Citizen Action Projects. A list of many citizen action projects that can be undertaken by any interested group.

Public Citizen Health Research Group's list of reports and publications includes information in the areas of food and drugs, occupational safety and health, pesticides, product safety, health care delivery, and how to get a copy of your health records.

Toll-free hotline numbers. A complete guide to all federal agencies designed to help and inform consumers.

Airline Passenger Rights. Information on your rights as an airline passenger, including how to deal with an airline-related problem. Write to ACAP (Aviation Consumer Action Project), P.O. Box 19029, Washington, D.C. 20036.

Freedom of Information. Pamphlet on the Freedom of Information Act and how to use it. Send SASE (self-addressed stamped envelope) to Freedom of Information Clearinghouse, P.O. Box 19367, Washington, D.C. 20036.

Pension Rights. Information on the rights of employees, retirees, and spouses under the new private pension reform law. Send SASE to the Pension Rights Center, 1346 Connecticut Avenue, N.W., Room 1019, Washington, D.C., 20036.

Human Rights and the Elderly. Information on programs involved with agism and other special projects. Send a first-class stamp to the Grey Panthers, 3700 Chestnut Street, Phildelphia, PA, 19104.

People and Taxes. Monthly newspaper of the Public Citizen's Tax Reform Research Group. Include a first-class stamp.

Critical Mass Newspaper covering nuclear power information and activity. Write to *Critical Mass,* P.O. Box 1538, Washington, D.C., 20013. Please include a first-class stamp.

People and Energy, CPSI Quarterly, The Nutrition Newsletter, and publications list. Newsletter from the Center for Science in the Public Interest. Send SASE to Center for Science in the Public Interest, 1757 S. Street, N.W., Washington, D.C., 20009.

In addition to the aforementioned publications, the following are some other helpful publications:

A monthly newsletter, *Cose Update,* is offered by:

Council of Smaller
   Enterprises of the
   Greater Cleveland
   Growth Association
690 Union Commerce
   Building
Cleveland, OH 44115
(216)621-3300

The Family Business Forum is the newsletter of the National Family Business Council. As the "voice of family business," this publication discusses important issues that affect the small business owner/managers. It also keeps its membership informed of the happenings within the organization on a local and national level. Write:

National Family Business
   Council
3916 Detroit Boulevard
W. Bloomfield, MI 48033

National Memo is a monthly newsletter that provides timely information on economic and business issues and events. *The*

SMALL BUSINESS PUBLICATIONS

Annual Subscription Price	Frequency	Magazine	Advertising Accepted	Hero
$48.00	Monthly	The Business Owner 50 Jericho Tpke. Jericho, NY 11753	No	Thomas J. Martin

The Business Owner is getting better editorially since the recent repurchase of the magazine by Tom Martin from the Transamerican Media Corporation, in Riverton, CT. Although Martin and his co-founder, Mark Gustafson, still write it, they are now investing more editorial time to produce quality work.

$15.00	Monthly	Venture Magazine 35 W. 45th Street New York, NY 10037	Yes	Joe Giarraputo

Venture Magazine is geared toward the individual who is starting his or her own business, and it best serves the $0 to $1 million business

$18.00	Monthly	Inc. Magazine 38 Commercial Wharf Boston, MA 02110	Yes	Bernard Goldhirsh

The focus of *Inc. Magazine* is directed to the market of managers of small businesses in the range of $1 million to $25 million.

Annual Subscription Price	Frequency	Magazine	Advertising Accepted	Hero
$36.00	Monthly	*Entrepreneur* 631 Wilshire Blvd. Santa Monica, CA 90401	Yes	Chase Revel

Entrepreneur is an opportunity magazine focusing on retailing and the retail trades. To receive it, you must be a member of the International Entrepreneurial Association (IEA).

$48.00	Monthly	*Small Business Report* 550 Hartnell St. Monterey, CA 93940	No	Gene E. Mattauch

Small Business Report is a pleasant, helpful and non-controversial magazine.

$42.00	Monthly	*The Professional Report* 118 Brook St. Scarsdale, NY 10503	No	John L. Springer

The *Professional Report* is basically a tax and management newsletter of well-established quality. It has been around much longer than any of the newsletters, and it is an excellent value.

$14.00	Bimonthly	*In Business* 18 So. 7th Street Emmaus, PA 18049	Yes	Jerome Goldstein

In Business is a new magazine with a combination of nature and small business, somewhat of an entrepreneur's "mother earth catalog." It is given free to members of the Support Service Alliance of New York.

$28.00	Bimonthly	*Journal of Applied Management* 1200 Mt. Diablo Blvd. Walnut Creek, CA 94596	Yes	John Stickler

Journal of Applied Management was originally founded by Bob Roth and is now owned by John Stickler. It is making a transition from being geared toward consultants to being geared toward the entrepreneur.

$97.00	Bimonthly	*New Venture Newsletter* George Spencer Observer Publishing Co. Canal Square Washington, D.C. 20007	No	George Spencer

New Venture Newsletter is geared toward successful business people who want to branchout into a wider range of business endeavors. It gives names and addresses to contact for information on promising ventures.

Corporate Guide to Minority Vendors is a resource manual for use by corporate executives and minority entrepreneurs to strengthen the communications network between the two sectors. The NBL also maintains a file of minority vendors and a comprehensive list of corporate procurement and purchasing agents for constituents. Write:

> National Business League
> 4324 Georgia Avenue,
>   N.W.
> Washington, D.C. 20011
> (202)829-5900

The Voice of Small Business is a monthly newsletter for small business owners/managers in all industries, trades, or professions. It deals generally with news of interest to small business relating to legislative and governmental activities in Washington. It is the membership newsletter of the National Small Business Association, a nonprofit and nonpartisan organization dedicated to the preservation and expansion of the small business sector of the economy. Write:

> National Small Business
>   Association
> 1225 19th Street, N.W.
> Washington, D.C. 20036

For the newsletter, *Voice of Small Business,* write:

> Voice of Small Business
> 1605 K Street, N.W.
> Washington, D.C. 20006
> (202)296-7400

The newsletter of the Chamber of Commerce of the United States is called *Washington Report.* Most of its subscribers are business people, and the majority of its articles are geared to information about federal policies and programs that can affect their firms and the economy. Write:

> Washington Report
> Chamber of Commerce of
>   the United States

1615 H Street, N.W.
Washington, D.C. 20062

Your local chamber of commerce can also be a source of valuable assistance, including information about plant or storage locations and financing. It is most quickly located via the local telephone directory.

M. Sources of Capital

How to raise capital for a growing enterprise is a fundamental question. The very nature of the venture capital industry has changed dramatically with the advent of Small Business Investment Companies (SBICs) launched by the Small Business Administration (SBA).

Locating sources of available venture capital can be both time consuming and frustrating if you don't know where to go or whom to contact. We have compiled the following comprehensive list of venture capital sources to aid you in your search.

SBA

SBA. The United States Small Business Administration is an independent, federal agency that was created by Congress in 1953 to assist, counsel, and champion American small businesses. The agency provides prospective, new, and established members of the small business community with financial assistance, management training and counseling, and help in getting a fair share of government contracts through over 100 offices throughout the nation.

SBIC. Small Business Investment Corporations are licensed, regulated, and in certain cases, financed by the SBA. They supply venture capital and long-term financing to small businesses for expansion, modernization, and sound financing for their organizations.

MESBIC. Minority Enterprise Small Business Investment Corporations have been incorporated into SBICs. They exist only to assist small business concerns owned and managed by socially or economically disadvantaged persons.

For more information about the services that the SBA provides, consult the Yellow Pages for the office nearest you or write:

SBA
1441 L Street, N.W.
Washington, D.C. 20005

SBIC Division
SBA
1441 L Street, N.W.
Washington, D.C. 20005

A Small Business Investment Company (SBIC) is a licensee of the federal government charged with making investments in small entrepreneurial ventures. A MESBIC is an SBIC that does the same thing for businesses with strong minority group interests. The way it works is simple. A pool of money is established (currently a minimum of $500,000 for an SBIC, $300,000 for a MESBIC), and then the manager of the pool of money applies to the SBIC division of the Small Business Administration (SBA) for an SBIC license. Once the pool of money qualifies for an SBIC license, you can accomplish the following:

1. A loan of between 3:1 and 4:1 times the amount in the pool of equity funds, you can leverage the equity by 3 or 4 times with an SBA loan.
2. The loan will be subordinated to bank debt. Consequently, with the total capital you should be able to borrow several million dollars on a short term basis from the banks.
3. The loan will be unsecured and all investors will have limited liabilities.
4. The loan will be a balloon payment loan with interest only payable.
5. The interest rate is currently three points under prime rate.

These features are a few of the incentives to reach the minimum targets of paid investment capital. There are some disadvantages to an SBIC and it is not a panacea, but the advantages often outweigh the disadvantages. One disadvantage is that any investment is limited to 20% of the paid-in capital ($500,000). Hence you could invest only up to $100,000 on any single deal. A second disadvantage is the paperwork that the SBA creates to prevent fraud in distribution of their funds.

Approximately 60% of the SBIC financing by number (and a little higher by dollars) are first or initial financings. This has been a fairly constant pattern for SBICs over the years. About half of the SBIC dollar financing is in the form of straight debt versus straight equity. The average interest on the debt in 1979 was just under 13% annually. The SBICs have an interest ceiling of 15% and rather than charge excessive interest, they are motivated to opt for equity in the form of warrants along with a debt financing.

The United States Small Business Administration (SBA) publishes on a quarterly basis a complete listing of SBICs as well as minority enterprise small business investment companies (MESBICs), listing name, address, and size category. Write:

    SBA Investment
      Divisions
    1441 L Street, N.W.
    Washington, D.C. 20416

    American Association of
      MESBICs
    1413 K Street, N.W., 13th
      Floor
    Washington, D.C. 20005
    (202)347-8600

The AAMESBIC newsletter is sent monthly to about 1,000 subscribers.

BANKS

Foreign-owned banks. The rapid expansion of foreign-owned banks in the United States is due primarily to the devaluation of the United States dollar and their ability to avoid United States banking regulations. They are allowed to open branches outside of their counties (United States banks are not), and they are not required to tie up funds in the Federal Reserve system. These foreign-owned banks fall under state banking regulations. The banks are most often found in metropolitan areas. Suggested banks to contact are Britain's Barclay Bank, the Bank of Montreal, or the Japanese, Swiss, or French banks. We suggest you consult your local Yellow Pages for the foreign-owned bank nearest you.

Two-tier lending. A major change in commercial bank lending was triggered by the heroes of small business at the Mellon National Bank in Pittsburgh, PA. They began offering small businesses a borrowing rate below the prime rate. They did this in times of money shortages (now) to help entrepreneurs, and they deserve pioneering recognition! For an up-to-date list of banks that offer a two-tier lending rate that is revised monthly write:

> Milton D. Stewart
> Chief Counsel for
>   Advocacy
> SBA
> 1441 L Street, N.W.
> Washington, D.C. 20005

Actually, Herbert A. Biern, Stewart's assistant, compiles these lists; his telephone number is (202) 653-6998. The list dated January 22, 1979 had 33 banks that offered special deals to small companies.

T.H.E. Insurance Company. The role of T.H.E. Insurance Company is to write an insurance policy to protect a lender against bankruptcy. They essentially appraise the collateral asset and insure to repossess it from a lender at the assessed rates. The value of T.H.E. policy allows more capital to be secured from existing lenders. It often happens that an asset or inventory can be borrowed against although it was given zero valuation by a bank because of T.H.E. insurance.

Lending institutions prefer to loan money against collateral because they maintain the option of liquidating the collateral to repay the loan. The table below is the rule of thumb for what can be loaned against different forms of collateral from the balance sheet of an entrepreneurial venture.

	Percentage to be Loaned Against
Accounts Receivable	75% − 80% under 90 days
Inventory	10% − 20%
Fixed Assets	70% − 80% market values

In practice, the actual ratios are even more pronounced. In other words, banks prefer not to lend against inventory as contrasted to lending against receivables.

In turn, easily liquidated, fixed assets are the most attractive type of collateral (automobiles), and they usually command both a high percentage of their lendable market value as well as a subsequently lower interest rate.

A lender is basically unsure of an inventory's value until it is converted to cash by being sold. That's the underlying reason that lenders shy away from accepting inventory of certain types of fixed assets as collateral for a loan. Thus, the role of T.H.E. Insurance Company is to write an insurance policy to protect a lender against bankruptcy. They essentially appraise the collateral asset and insure to repossess it from a lender at the assessed rates. Rather than paying off the insurance policy on a death, the policy is paid upon default in the loan. Here's how it works:

1. T.H.E. appraises the assets to be pledged, including both inventory and fixed assets.
2. T.H.E. will then issue an insurance policy for the amount of their appraisal.
3. The company hands this policy over to the lender and then borrows 100% of the value of the policy in a loan.
4. If the company defaults, T.H.E. takes title to the collateral and sells it. The lender is paid in full using T.H.E.'s credit and capital to be reimbursed.

What does all this insurance protection cost?

1. Appraisal fee: minimum amount: $1,000. This is for the appraisal and it is 1% of the appraised value of the collateral plus out-of-pocket (travel) expenses.

2. A 2% add-on interest rate on the outstanding loan balance, not on the full appraisal of the collateral. The premium interest rate of 2% is charged only on what's borrowed or what is at risk.

The value of T.H.E. policy allows more capital to be secured from existing lenders. On the one hand, a lender will typically allow only 10% of inventory value to be used as loan collateral, with a policy the inventory allowed as collateral might be above 50% of its value, depending upon T.H.E.'s assessment. This often allows a two or three times greater amount to be loaned against an asset.

An asset or inventory can often be borrowed against when it was given zero valuation by a bank because of the T.H.E. formula. On a theoretical basis, the lending interest rate can be reduced if you can convince the lender of the merits and security of the guarantee. In effect, given the policy, the lender should advance funds on T.H.E.'s credit, not the credit of your entrepreneurial venture.

In practice, you are seldom ever able to negotiate the bank interest rate lower by securing a T.H.E. guarantee and, in total, you are paying 5 to 6% above prime rate for this type of lending. If your entrepreneurial venture can service debt, write:

Mr. Ed Shifman, V.P.
T.H.E. Insurance
  Company
52 Church Street
Boston, MA 02116
(617)357-5220

FARMERS HOME LOAN

The SBA is supposedly the government agency charged with helping the entrepreneur, but in practice other federal agencies also provide a great deal of help. The FmHa is the loan program of the Farmers Home Administration which offers guaranteed loans to growing businesses. Unlike the SBA's program with a $500,000 ceiling, the FmHa loan program has no ceiling. In fact, loans have ranged from $7,000 to $33 million with an average of about $900,000.

The FmHa loan gives preference to distressed areas and rural communities of less than 25,000 inhabitants. It will loan money for any worthwhile business purpose. The minimum equity requirement is 10% and, if your venture can be shown to be job-creating, your loan has a greater chance of approval. Unlike the SBA, you do not have to prove to be an unbankable company to secure a FmHa loan. The loans are for fairly long terms, 30 years for construction, 15 years for equipment, and 7 years for working capital. The interest rate is about the same as can be negotiated with a bank, but the FmHa has a one-time fee that is calculated by multiplying 1% of the principal loan amount by the percentage of the guarantee. Even given the one-time fee, the good standing of the U.S. government stands behind the guaranteed portions of the loan, and the interest rate eventually negotiated often effects these favorable considerations.

Why not write the FmHa in care of the (USDA) United States Dept. of Agriculture, Washington, DC 20250, or you could look in your nearest largest city Yellow Pages for one of the 1800 county offices. Look under US Government—Agriculture.

EDA FUNDS

If your company needs funds to expand or strengthen an existing business, you may be eligible for federal funds without knowing it. The federal government has designated two-thirds of all counties in the U.S. as "economically depressed." If you're located in one of these areas, you may apply for a loan under the special program of the Economic Development Administration. To qualify for such a loan, a company must show that it has been unable to borrow under similar terms and conditions from other sources. There is no limit on the amount that may be requested. Most of the loans are under $1 million, or $10,000 per job created or saved.

On direct loans for fixed assets, or where there is mortgagable collateral, the interest rate is currently under 10%. EDA would provide up to 65% of the total funds, but the applicant has to put at least 15% of his own and get 5% from his state or a nongovernmental community organization, such as a Community Development Corporation. The repayment time is usually the useful life of the fixed assets. The interest rate on a direct loan for working capital or for less mortgagable assets is usually only a ¼% higher than fixed assets.

A list of economically depressed areas, the loan application form, and other details of the loan program can be obtained from any of EDA's six regional offices. For the address of the office nearest you, write or call:

Office of Business
  Development
Economic Development
  Administration
Room 7876
14th & Constitution
  Avenue, N.W.
Washington, D.C., 20230
(202)377-2000

BUSINESS DEVELOPMENT CORPORATION

The purpose of Business Development Corporations is to attract and retain business in their respective states, and thus increase employment. Although they sound like government agencies, they are not. BDCs operate within a state. Business development corporations are specifically designed to provide long-term capital to small businesses. With capital tough to get today, it is a good idea to become familiar with your state BDC. For further information contact your local chamber of commerce or write to:

Industrial Development
  Corporation of Florida
801 North Magnolia
  Avenue, Suite 218
Orlando, FL 32803

First Arkansas
  Development Finance
  Corporation
910 Pyramid Life
  Building

Little Rock, AR 72201
(501)374-9247
Alaska State
  Development
  Corporation
Pouch D
Juneau, AK 99811

Statewide California Business & Indus. Dev. Corp.
717 Lido Park Drive
Newport Beach, CA 92663
(714)675-8030

Connecticut Development Credit Corporation
99 Colony Street, P.O. Box 714
Meriden, CT 06450
(203)235-3327

Business Development Corporation of Georgia, Inc.
822 Healey Building
Atlanta, GA 30303
(404)577-5715

Iowa Business Development Credit Corp.
247 Jewett Building
Des Moines, IA 50309
(515)282-9546

Kansas Development Credit Corp.
First National Bank Tower, Suite 620
One Townsite Plaza
Topeka, KS 66603
(913)235-3437

Business Development Corp. of Kentucky
1940 Commonwealth Building
Louisville, KY 40202
(502)584-3519

Development Credit Corp. of Maine

P.O. Box 262
Manchester, ME 04351
(207)724-3507

Development Credit Corporation of Maryland
1301 First National Bank Building
Baltimore, MD 21202
(301)685-6454

Massachusetts Business Development Corp.
One Boston Place, Suite 3607
Boston, MA 02108
(617)723-7515

First Missouri Development Finance Corp.
302 Adams Street, P.O. Box 252
Jefferson City, MO 65101
(314)635-0138

Development Credit Corp. of Montana
P.O. Box 916
Helena, MT 59601
(406)442-3850

Business Development Corporation of Nebraska
Suite 1044, Stuart Building
Lincoln, NE 68508
(402)474-3855

New Hampshire Business Development Corp.
10 Fort Eddy Road

Concord, NH 03301
(603)224-1432

New York Business
  Development Corp.
41 State Street
Albany, NY 12207
(518)463-2268

Business Development
  Corp. of N. Carolina
505 Oberlin Rd., P.O.
  Box 10665
Raleigh, NC 27605
(919)828-2331

North Dakota State Dev.
  Credit Corp.
Box 1212
Bismark, ND 58501
(701)223-2288

Oklahoma Business
  Development Corp.
1018 United Founders
  Life Tower
Oklahoma City, OK 73112
(405)840-1674

RIDC Industrial
  Development Fund
Union Trust Building
Pittsburgh, PA 15219
(717)234-3241

Southeastern
  Pennsylvania
  Development Fund
3 Penn Center Plaza
Philadelphia, PA 19102
(215)568-4677

Business Development
  Co. of Rhode Island
40 Westminster Street
Providence, RI 02903
(401)751-1000

Business Development
  Corp. of S. Carolina
Palmetto State Life
  Building
P.O. Box 11606
Columbia, SC 29211
(803)252-3759

Virginia Industrial
  Development Corp.
201 Mutual Building,
  P.O. Box 474
Richmond, VA 23204

Business Development
  Corp. of Eastern
  Washington
417 Hyde Building
Spokane, WA 99201
(509)838-2731

N. Venture Capital Resource Publications

The Capital Publishing Company was originally started by the late
Stanley Rubel in 1961 and was recently acquired by Stanley Pratt. It
has been the single clearinghouse for most industry-wide informa-

tion on venture capital. They offer several publications, including a monthly newsletter entitled *Venture Capital*, which highlights a number of useful areas of what's happening within the industry. *The Guide to Venture Capital Sources*, 4th edition, is the most valuable single source on venture capital ever published. Besides a nicely indexed listing of venture capital sources by state and by product group interest, the front half of this guide has several valuable articles. About $550 million is invested annually by about 450 professional venture capital firms with assets of about $3,000,000,-000. The directory lists 600 sources and is available for $49.50.

The Source Guide for Borrowing Capital by Leonard Smollen, Stanley Rubel, Mark Rollinson (1977) tells how to raise capital without having to give up any equity. There are 50 federal programs for financing small business handled by nine different government agencies. This includes the SBA, the FHA, and others. The directory also lists state agencies, commercial banks, insurance companies, commercial finance companies, leasing companies, and investors in industrial revenue bonds. It is a valuable directory.

The Guide to Selling a Business by Stanley Rubel (1977) lists about 1,500 acquisition-oriented corporations. In addition, about 100 companies are seeking leveraged buy-outs; also about 500 professional merger intermediaries are listed. This unique and valuable book available for $49.50.

For more information on these publications, write:

The Center for
  Entrepreneurial
  Managment, Inc.
311 Main Street
Worcester, Massachusetts
  01608
(617)755-0770

Capital Publishing
  Corporation
2 Laurel Avenue, Box 348
Wellesley Hills, MA 02181
(617)235-5405

The Center for Community and Economic Development (CCED), along with the Institute for New Enterprise Development (INED), has compiled *Sources of Capital for Community and Economic Development*, an excellent sourcebook on capital. In addition, the CCED offers a free bimonthly newsletter for interested parties. This group works to promote the concept of community based economic development. Write:

>   CCED/Cynthia Rose
>   639 Massachusetts
>   Avenue
>   Suite 316
>   Cambridge, MA 02139
>   (617)547-9695

The Directory of State and Federal Funds is a single source for basic data on the financial assistance programs of the 50 states and 12 federal agencies. This concise directory is the starting point for any business, large or small, that seeks to relocate or expand. The book helps management to "shop," compare, select, and discard a wide range of aid programs without collecting and sorting through mountains of promotional literature. Write:

>   Directory of State and
>   Federal Funds for
>   Business Development
>   Pilot Books
>   347 Fifth Avenue
>   New York, NY 10016

How and Where to Raise Venture Capital by Ted Nicholas (1978) is an excellent 68-page pamphlet on venture capital. Write:

>   Enterprise Publishing
>   Company
>   1300 Market Street
>   Wilmington, DE 19801

Another Booklet by Ted Nicholas is *Where the Money Is and How to Get It.*

How to Finance a Growing Business by Royce Diener is a book on capital security written from the viewpoint of the businessman-borrower. It not only describes what is available in the field of finance but also provides insight into what goes on in the lender's mind and by what standards the funding source operates. This is an exceedingly readable and understandable basic work on finance, including the more serious business of raising capital to start a company, keeping a growing concern solvent, financing the purchase of other companies, issuing securities and international finance. It is written from the viewpoint of the businessman. Write:

Frederick Fell Publishers,
    Inc.
386 Park Avenue, South
New York, NY 10016
(212)685-9017

The Business Research and Service Institute of the College of Business at Western Michigan University publishes a spiral bound book entitled *Johnson's Directory of Risk Capital for Small Business,* edited by James M. Johnson, Ph.D., a member of the finance faculty. This several hundred page listing and categorizing of venture capital lists 373 venture Firms. Write:

Professor James Johnson
Faculty of Finance
Western Michigan
    University
Kalamazoo, MI 49008

Venture Capital by John R. Dominquez (1974) includes a list of venture capital firms by investment limits. Write:

D.C. Heath Company
125 Spring Street
Lexington, MA 02173
(617)862-6650

Howard and Company publishes an excellent guide for borrowing capital. The *1978 Market for Risk Capital Directory* is $25.00 and the *Program for Successful Bank Borrowing* is $50.00. This is not a well-known source of venture capital information, but it is a good one. Write:

Graham Howard
Howard and Company

1529 Walnut Street, 5th
  Floor
Philadelphia, PA 19102
(215)603-8030

How to Raise Money to Make Money (The Executive's Guide to Financing a Business) is an excellent book that is easy to read and extremely comprehensive. The Institute for Business Planning, a subsidiary of Prentice-Hall, has some excellent material available for entrepreneurs. A monthly newsletter called *Closely Held Business* contains almost every known way to boost profits and generate personal wealth from a closely held business. Business, financial, and tax implications of buying, operating, expanding, selling, or terminating a business are discussed in this newsletter. Write:

Institute for Business
  Planning
IBP Plaza
Englewood Cliffs, NJ
  07632
(201)592-2040

A source of international venture capital offers a newsletter, *Finance International,* and several directories on venture capital. One of the directories is called *Guide to Corporate Borrowing: Sources and Rates.* Write:

Institute for International
  Research
95 Madison Avenue
New York, NY 10016

If you've ever tried to raise capital for a business venture, consider this book, *A Guide to Money Sources and How to Approach Them Successfully,* which covers such topics as various sources of loans, preparation of loan requests, government financing, and financial data and analysis as it relates to loans. The book is available from:

Kephart
  Communications, Inc.
901 Washington Street,

Suite 200
Alexandria, VA 22314

The following three books are available from B. Klein Publishing Company: (1) *Business Capital Sources:* Lists hundreds of firms, banks, mortgage lenders, etc., having capital available for business loans. Also gives many hints on running a business successfully. (2) *How and Where to Get Capital* gives information on over 4,500 organizations and foundations that make capital loans, with requirements for borrowing. It also supplies information on raising capital through venture and risk capital sources. (3) *Small Business Investment Company Directory and Handbook* lists more than 400 small business investment companies interested in various businesses; also gives recommended procedures for running a profitable business. Write:

B. Klein Publishing, Inc.
P.O. Box 8503
Coral Springs, FL 33065
(305)752-1708

The Money Market Directory lists the 4,600 largest institutional funds, their addresses, telephone numbers, amounts of money managed, and the money managers and investment counselors for each. These investors own securities with a market value of $1 trillion, with annual investment purchases and sales of $200 billion.

Money Market Directory
Money Market
  Directories, Inc.
370 Lexington Avenue
New York, NY 10070

The National Association of Small Business Investment Companies (SBICs) offers a twice-monthly newsletter from Washington, D.C. It is one of the better sources of what is happening within the venture capital industry.

NASBIC News
512 Washington Building
Washington, D.C. 20005

The NASBIC membership directory of 21 pages is free as well. The directory lists names, addresses, telephone numbers, key executives, and a code to distinguish: preferred limit for loans or investments, investment policy, industry preference. About 5,000 of these directories are given away annually. The approximate circulation of the semimonthly newsletter is 500. The newsletter is extremely helpful for keeping up with legislation effecting the venture capital industry.

The New England Venture Capital Directory, written by John McKiernan, is similar to the original book, but much more current, with a 1978 copyright. It lists about 100 of the most popular sources of venture capital around the country. However, its real strength lies in its commentaries about the Northeast venture groups. The second half of the book discusses entrepreneurs, business plans, and venture capitalists. Write:

> John McKiernan
> Management Association
> Box 230
> Chestnut Hill, MA 02167

A 134-page study by the Management Department at Boston College, entitled *Venture Capital—A Guidebook for New Enterprise*, is especially good for Northeastern Unite States businesses. Write:

> Superintendent of
>   Documents
> U.S. Government
>   Printing Office
> Re: Committee Print No.
>   75-292
> Washington, D.C. 20416

Leroy W. Sinclair edits a hard-cover book entitled *Venture Capital*, which offers details on all venture capital firms in the United States. In addition, he publishes a spiral-bound book entitled *The Business Plan*, which is a practical guide on how to write a business plan. Write:

> Technimetrics, Inc.
> 919 Third Avenue
> New York, NY 10022

Winthrop Brown &
Company
527 Madison Avenue
New York, NY 10022

Venture Capital in the United States: An Analysis (1972) is an excellent guide on risk capital and venture management as practiced by large corporations. Write:

Venture Development
Corporation
One Washington Street
Wellesley, MA 02181
(617)237-5080

Western Association of Venture Capitalists—Directory of Members, San Francisco, provides a list of members and periodic bulletins on West Coast ventures. Write:

Directory of Members
244 California Street
Room 700 San Francisco,
CA 94111
(415)781-6897

A Handbook of Business Finance and Capital Sources. This hard cover handbook has 460 pages and an excellent reference book on more than 1,000 capital sources. It contains information on financing techniques and instruments for both private and government sources of capital. It is a very detailed and well-presented reference book. It would be useful for anyone trying to raise capital. The price is $50.00 per copy. The author/editor is Dileep Rao, Ph.D., who was also India's number one ranked junior table tennis player. Not only is the author an academician, but also an entrepreneur by way of his self-published book. Write to:

Dileep Rao
InterFinance Corporation
305 Foshay Tower
Minneapolis, MN 55402
(612)338-8185

SOURCES OF CORPORATE VENTURE CAPITAL

Kenneth W. Rind, the principle in the Xerox Development Corporation, states that there has been a resurgence in corporate venture capital. The following list contains the industrial firms that have been most active in this resurgence:

Textron	Johnson & Johnson
Xerox	3M
Gould	Corning
Time	Dun & Bradstreet
Innoven-Monsanto/Emerson	Fairchild Camera
Exxon	CTS
Standard Oil of Indiana	Control Data
General Electric	Burroughs
Syntex	NCR
Motorola	TRW
Bolt Beranek & Newman, Inc.	National City Lines
Arthur D. Little	Telescience
Inco	

Foreign-based companies are also active in venture capital. They include:

Northern Telecom	Fujitsu
Siemens	Robert Bosch
Nippon Electric	Lucas Industries
Seiko	Jaegar
Oki	VDO
Mitsui	

O. Women Entrepreneurs

One of the great changes in the 1980s has been the emergence of the woman entrepreneur. The Women's Liberation Movement has brought women out of the home and into the work force. Now women understand the value and the importance of the start-your-own-business process, and they are beginning to become entrepreneurs at a much faster rate. In 1978 about 11% of all businesses were owned by women. However, more than half of the United States wealth is in the hands of females. Sources of help for women entrepreneurs are listed here; however, don't disregard the other sources of information that are equally valuable.

Women have specialized needs to help combat some of the natural forces that work against a woman in business. These sources of information are offered to help a woman combat these problems.

American Women's
  Economic Development
  Corporation
250 Broadway
New York, NY 10007

The Businesswoman's
  Letter
P.O. Box 337
Wall Street Station
New York, NY 10005

ORGANIZATIONS

The National Association for Female Executives, Inc. seeks out opportunities, provides information, arranges special offers, and offers information on extending your money power. Write:

NAFE Executive Office
32 East 39th Street
New York, NY 10016

NAFE Administrative
  Office
31 Jeremys Way
Annapolis, MD 21403
(301)267-0630

National Association of
  Women Business
  Owners

200 P Street, N.W., Suite
  511
Washington, D.C. 20036
(202)338-8966

More and more women are becoming entrepreneurs. Other sources
of help are available.

New England Women
  Business Owners
% SBANE
69 Hickory Drive
Waltham, MA 02154
(617)890-9070

New York Association of
  Women Business
  Owners/Enterprising
  Women
525 West End Avenue
New York, NY 10024
(A monthly newsletter is
  offered to subscribers.)

PUBLICATIONS

*Small Business Ideas for
  Women and How to Get
  Started,* by Terri Hilton.
Pilot Books
347 Fifth Avenue
New York, NY 10016

The Woman's Guide to Starting a Business, by Claudia Jessup and
Genie Chipps, 1978. This two-part guide is concerned with the
special problems that women face when establishing a business.
Part I consists of basic information on getting started, and Part II is
a collection of interviews of successful women entrepreneurs. Write:

Holt, Rinehart & Winston
383 Madison Avenue
New York, NY 10017

A montly, 12-page digest of affirmative action news, *Womanpower* is a newsletter designed to keep employers up to date with the laws, government regulations, suits, and court decisions that affect the employment of women of all races, ages, religions, and ethnic origins. Write:

Betsy Hogan Association
222 Rawson Road
Brookline, MA 02146
(617)232-0066

Women Entrepreneurs
P.O. Box 26738
San Francisco, CA 94126
Contact: Sue Easton,
   (415)474-3000

Women-Owned Businesses, 1972, 1976, provides basic economic data on businesses owned by all women and on minority firms owned by women. Data include number of firms, gross receipts, and number of paid employees, listed geographically by industry, size of firm, and legal form of organization of firm.

The Entrepreneurial Woman, Newsweek Books, is a new book recently written by Sandra Winston. It is a 740-page easy reader. Sandra is both a marriage counselor and a business consultant. Her book focuses on the people side of the issue with a great understanding of women but with less insight into the process of launching entrepreneurial ventures. One of the chapters, entitled "How to Be Assertive" leads the reader to believe she is talking to would-be entrepreneurs who are presently housewives. Her writing style is excellent, and she does have a good bibliography.

Speaking of bibliographies, here is a great one on the subject. The title is *Women in the Economy,* a 40-page bibliography compiled in 1979. It is a source of information on careers and education in business for women. It was prepared as a project by the Empire State College Center for Business and Economic Information with the assistance of the Hauppauge unit of the Empire State College. Write:

George S. Dawson,
  Director
Empire State College
Long Island Regional
  Center
Old Westbury State
  University of New York
Box 130
Old Westbury, NY 11568

Septima Palm has a range of services for the female entrepreneur including a new book called the *Cinderella Syndrome*. Write:

Success Series
Box 2096
Sarasota, FL 33578
(813)349-4634

Dottie Walters is another woman who has been extremely successful in promoting the female entrepreneur. Write:

Dottie Walters
600 West Foothill Blvd.
Glendora, CA 91740
(213)335-0218

Index